TEACHING MATHEMATICS
VISUALLY & ACTIVELY

Education at SAGE

SAGE is a leading international publisher of journals, books, and electronic media for academic, educational, and professional markets.

Our education publishing includes:

- accessible and comprehensive texts for aspiring education professionals and practitioners looking to further their careers through continuing professional development

- inspirational advice and guidance for the classroom

- authoritative state of the art reference from the leading authors in the field

Find out more at: **www.sagepub.co.uk/education**

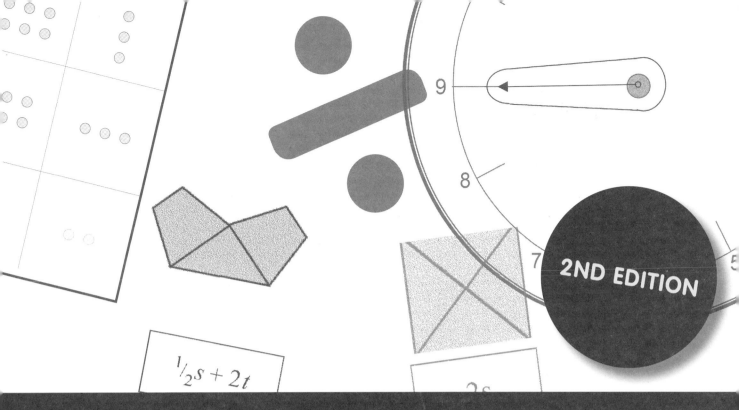

2ND EDITION

$\frac{1}{2}s + 2t$

TEACHING MATHEMATICS
VISUALLY & ACTIVELY

TANDI CLAUSEN-MAY

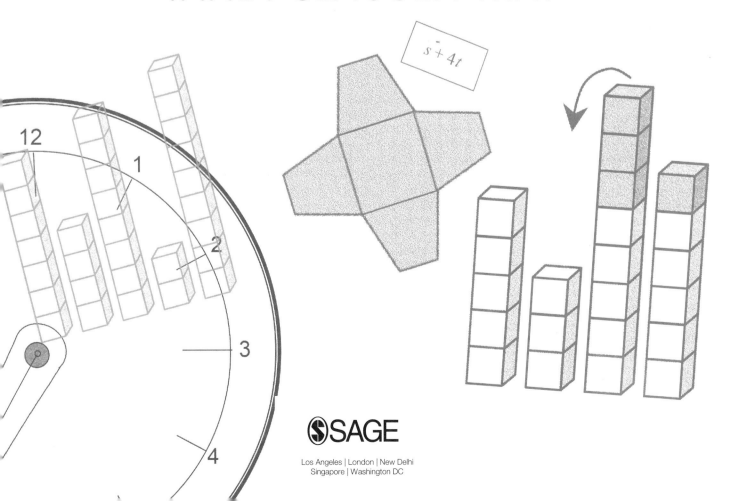

$^{-}s + 4t$

§SAGE

Los Angeles | London | New Delhi
Singapore | Washington DC

Los Angeles | London | New Delhi
Singapore | Washington DC

SAGE Publications Ltd
1 Oliver's Yard
55 City Road
London EC1Y 1SP

SAGE Publications Inc.
2455 Teller Road
Thousand Oaks, California 91320

SAGE Publications India Pvt Ltd
B 1/I 1 Mohan Cooperative Industrial Area
Mathura Road
New Delhi 110 044

SAGE Publications Asia-Pacific Pte Ltd
3 Church Street
#10-04 Samsung Hub
Singapore 049483

Editor: Jude Bowen
Assistant editor: Miriam Davey
Production editor: Thea Watson
Copyeditor: Jill Birch
Proofreader: Elaine Leek
Indexer: Anne Solamito
Marketing manager: Lorna Patkai
Cover design: Wendy Scott
Typeset by: C&M Digitals (P) Ltd, Chennai, India
Printed in India by: Replika Press Pvt Ltd

First published 2005 as *Teaching Maths to Pupils with Different Learning Styles*
Reprinted 2007, 2009, 2010, 2011

Library of Congress Control Number: 2012955612

British Library Cataloguing in Publication data

A catalogue record for this book is available from the British Library

ISBN 978-1-4462-4085-4
ISBN 978-1-4462-4086-1 (pbk)

Dedication

This book is dedicated to my husband, John Baker May, for his unstinting support and encouragement of everything that I have sought to do.

CONTENTS

RESOURCES ON THE CD

List of Further Reading and Resources in the Book

Chapter 2 The Concept of Number
Resource Sheet
      RS 2-1 *Slavonic Abacus Grids*

Chapter 3 Models for Multiplication and Division
Mathematical PowerPoints
      PP 3-1 *Dotty Arrays*
      PP 3-2 *Area Model for Multiplication*
      PP 3-3 *Two Models for Division*
Resource Sheet
      RS 3-1 *Array Cards*
Posters
      P 3-1 *Dotty Arrays: Array Cards – Teacher's Set*
      P 3-2 *Slavonic Multiplication*
      P 3-3 *Handy Multiplication*

Chapter 4 Place Value and Decimals
Mathematical PowerPoints
      PP 4-1 *Whole Number Place Value 1 – Cubes, Sticks and Slabs*
      PP 4-2 *Whole Number Place Value 2 – Modelling Numbers*
      PP 4-3 *Whole Number Place Value 3 – Multiplying by 10*
      PP 4-4 *Decimal Place Value*
Resource Sheets
      RS 4-1 *Folding Number*
      RS 4-2 *Decimal Slide Holder*
      RS 4-3 *Decimal Slide Number*

Chapter 5 Fractions
Mathematical PowerPoints
      PP 5-1 *n n^{ths} Make a Whole One*
      PP 5-2 *Fractions and Repeating Patterns*
Resource Sheets
      RS 5-1 *Large Fraction Clock*
      RS 5-2 *Small Fraction Clocks*

Chapter 6 Ratio, Proportion and Percentages
No resources on the CD

Chapter 7 Algebra
Mathematical PowerPoints
>PP 7-1 *Balancing*
>PP 7-2 *Tangram Algebra*
>PP 7-3 *Multiplying out Brackets*

Resource Sheet
>RS 7-1 *Tangram Tiles*

Chapter 8 Angle
Mathematical PowerPoints
>PP 8-1 *What is an Angle?*
>PP 8-2 *Degrees*
>PP 8-3 *External Angles*
>PP 8-4 *Internal Angles Part 1*
>PP 8-5 *Internal Angles Part 2*

Resource Sheet
>RS 8-1 *Angle Machine*

Chapter 9 Perimeter, Area and Volume
Mathematical PowerPoints
>PP 9-1 *Tangram Areas*
>PP 9-2 *Areas of Straight-Sided Shapes*

Chapter 10 Circles and Time
Mathematical PowerPoints
>PP 10-1 *Circumference of a Circle*
>PP 10-2 *Area of a Circle*

Resource Sheet
>RS 10-1 *Cyclic Calendar*

Chapter 11 Data Handling
Mathematical PowerPoints
>PP 11-1 *Polyomino Scatter Graph*
>PP 11-2 *Brothers and Sisters*

Conclusion
Poster
>P 12-1 *Cartoon*

ACKNOWLEDGEMENTS

My sincere thanks go to my sister Barbary Love and my old colleague Adrian Woodthorpe, for all their support with the first version of this book; to my editor, Jude Bowen, and her assistant, Miriam Davey, for keeping the flame alive; and to the unknown but greatly valued reviewers whose comments on the revised manuscripts provided so much encouragement and sound advice.

Tandi Clausen-May is an experienced teacher and educational researcher, with a particular interest in making mathematics accessible and engaging to all learners in every school. She has developed a wide range of teaching and learning materials for use in the UK and internationally, and has been involved in the development of both school and national mathematics assessment at primary and at secondary level. Tandi writes regularly about aspects of mathematics teaching, learning and assessment for academic and professional journals, and she runs professional development workshops for mathematics educators. She plays an active part in the Association of Teachers of Mathematics, and she is a Fellow of the Chartered Institute of Educational Assessors.

Tandi is currently working as an International Consultant in Mathematics Education at the National Curriculum Development Centre in Kampala. The Centre, supported by Cambridge Education, is undertaking the Curriculum, Assessment and Examinations (CURASSE) reform programme to review and revise all aspects of curriculum and assessment in Ugandan lower secondary schools.

CHAPTER 1

Introduction

Some key concepts

- This book is about teaching mathematics to learners who have learning *differences*, not learning *difficulties*.

- Children who think and learn visually and actively often struggle with a school curriculum that relies heavily on print.

- Visual and kinaesthetic mathematics are under-valued in the classroom.

- The development of 'pictures in the mind' can help all learners to understand key mathematical concepts.

- A visual and kinaesthetic approach is worthwhile only if it is based on understanding.

a) Differences and Difficulties

This book is about teaching mathematics to learners who take in information and ideas visually and actively. These learners have learning *differences*, not learning *difficulties*. Teaching and learning in our schools has always been, and continues to be, heavily reliant on print. Literacy is all, whether learners are working from a book or with a screen: other ways of thinking – visual, kinaesthetic, practical – are discounted in the classroom. To become teachers, students must jump over a long series of hurdles, formal and informal, at school, at college and at university. These hurdles consist of print-based activities and assessments that demand a high level of linguistic and symbolic thought but take little account of other ways of thinking and learning. As a result, teachers are rarely selected for their visual or kinaesthetic abilities as these have little impact on their academic achievement. It is their verbal and numerical skills that have opened the doors to success, not their spatial skills. This may make it difficult for teachers to recognise spatial ability in their learners, so real strengths and aptitudes are neglected as children are forced to struggle with a curriculum which is largely presented through printed materials that they find hard to access.

Because the curriculum is so heavily print-based, 'proper' school mathematics is defined by what can be printed in a book, and preferably in text. Definitions and proofs that depend on models or dynamic geometry rather than on symbols are second best. So, for example,

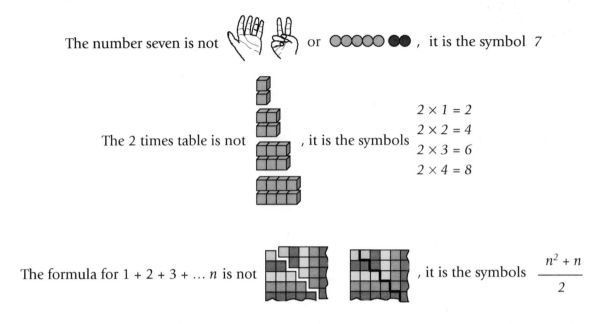

The number seven is not [hands] or [circles] , it is the symbol *7*

The 2 times table is not [blocks] , it is the symbols

$2 \times 1 = 2$
$2 \times 2 = 4$
$2 \times 3 = 6$
$2 \times 4 = 8$

The formula for $1 + 2 + 3 + \dots n$ is not [grids] , it is the symbols $\dfrac{n^2 + n}{2}$

Pictures and models may be used to support learning, especially in the early stages, but the end point is symbolic. Symbols are easier to print, and they always take precedence over visual or kinaesthetic representations.

But to some children, the numbers and symbols on the page are just squiggles. These learners can *see* that seven is five plus two, or that twice two two's will fit together to make four two's, or that the sum of the first *n* counting numbers is half the area of a rectangle with sides *n* and *n* + 1. They may not be able to put it into words, but they can see it, and perhaps draw it. But the printed symbols, the squiggles, are meaningless. It is for these children, and for their teachers, that this book and CD have been put together.

b) Visual, Auditory, Kinaesthetic

So – what is 'visual and active mathematics'? How can we go about teaching 'visually and actively'?

There are nearly as many theories about learning as there are researchers writing about it. Steve Chinn offers a useful summary of 'thinking styles in mathematics', and shows how, to some extent at least, the different models overlap and interrelate (Chinn, 2004: 59–75). But for general classroom use the VAK model – Visual, Auditory, Kinaesthetic – will serve us well. It is at least as old as Confucius –

I hear, and I forget;

I see, and I remember;

I do, and I understand.

This model is quite straightforward – and it works in real classrooms, not just in lecture halls – so it can provide the theoretical structure we need for the ideas and activities discussed in this book.

The phrase *kinaesthetic learning* is sometimes taken to mean any activity that involves the use of apparatus. This may be considered particularly appropriate for 'slow learners' – at least they will have something to *do* in their mathematics lessons. But if the focus of the teaching is primarily on the correct use of the apparatus, rather than on the mathematical understanding that the apparatus is designed to develop, then it may have very limited impact. Learners will just follow the instructions to use the equipment, without necessarily relating what they are doing to mathematics.

Kinaesthetic learning calls for a lot more than a pile of cubes or a pair of scissors and some card. It involves using your whole being, engaging all your senses to feel or imagine what is happening. Visual, aural and kinaesthetic learning are all intertwined: together they can lay down a memory – of movement, feeling, sight and sound – that will be recalled as a total experience, not just as a recited chant. For example, when I think about the number seven I can *feel* the seven in all the fingers of one hand and two fingers of the other. When I factorise, I can imagine pulling apart *eight* to make two sets of *two twos*. And I can feel myself breaking up a 10 by 11 unit rectangle into two halves to find the sum of the first ten counting numbers, $1 + 2 + 3 + \ldots + 10$. Because I have done all these activities, and have understood the mathematics that they represent, I do not need to actually hold up my fingers or make blocks of cubes in order to recall them. But what I recall is most certainly not a chant or a formula: it is more like a moving picture – a sort of waking dream. This, I believe, is kinaesthetic learning.

It is essential, too, that visual images are fully supported by kinaesthetic movement. Computers have provided an incredibly powerful tool that enables us to present our ideas visually, with dynamic images that can convey key concepts meaningfully and memorably. But there may be a temptation to do away with the physical equipment altogether – the piles of cubes, the scissors and card, and all the other bits and pieces that help us to create and share representations of key mathematical concepts. After all, we have an unlimited supply of cubes on the screen, and they never roll off the table and get lost. It would be much more straightforward to rely on those. But our learners need the real cubes. They need to handle them, and to actually create and break up the models for themselves. You will find lots of dynamic images in the files on the CD that accompanies this book, and they should be helpful. But they will not – they cannot – replace the contents of the equipment cupboard. You need both.

All the learners in a mathematics classroom – like all the teachers – are able to think visually and kinaesthetically to a greater or lesser degree. There is not a clear-cut divide between spatial thinkers and those who think in words and symbols. The chief difference lies, not in the ability of different learners to think spatially or numerically, but in the value that is placed on the different ways of thinking. But how can teachers spot visual and kinaesthetic ability, and identify learners who are likely to learn more effectively through models that they can construct and take apart, and through 'pictures in the mind'? Teachers may well notice the visual and kinaesthetic thinkers in their classroom by their responses to different types of mathematical task. These are the learners who have found all the nets of a cube before most of the rest of the class have grasped what a net is – but for whom 'seven eights' are 'forty-three' on Tuesday, and 'sixty-two' on Wednesday. With a print-based curriculum they rarely shine – but just occasionally they take everyone (including, quite possibly, themselves) by surprise with their ability to just *see* the solution to a problem with which other learners are struggling.

Any teaching idea, no matter how inspirational, can be reduced to 'rote learning' – *I hear and I forget*. On the other hand, the dreariest exercise might be transformed into a basis for real understanding by a teacher who can unpack the underlying concepts and help learners to understand and use them. The most effective mathematical thinkers are flexible: they try different approaches to the problem in hand, finding out what works best and relating each new idea to what they already know. The *hearing*, the *seeing* and the *doing* support one another, as the pictures, models and activities give meaning to the spoken or written definitions and procedures. Learners may adopt different ways of thinking as they first explore and understand, and then rehearse and apply, each new concept. But for learners who think more easily in pictures and movement than in words and symbols, *seeing* and *doing* may offer access to key mathematical ideas, while too much time spent *hearing* may slam the door shut.

c) Pictures in the Mind

Some people can follow a set of directions easily, but others find it much more helpful to have a visual image. For example, one person might find it easy to follow a written description of a route:

> *Turn left out of the gate, and walk to the T-junction at the end of the road. There you should cross the road and turn right. Take the first left turn, and walk past the school and across the crossroads. You will come to another crossroads, with a church on the corner; there you must turn left. Walk about fifty metres down the road, and the house you want, number 33, is on the right opposite the post box.*

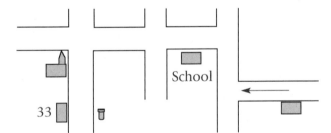

But another might prefer a map. They find the map easier than the linear series of instructions to understand and to follow, and they can recall it more easily when they need to find their way again along the same route.

In the mathematics classroom diagrams may be used, but, as we have seen, they are generally subservient to the written, symbolic forms. A map (or its equivalent) is rarely considered to be enough on its own – while a written formula, or a set of rules for carrying out a procedure, can stand alone. Learners who can take in and remember a series of instructions, or a formula, or the 'rules' for adding fractions or finding the sine of an angle, achieve high grades and feel successful. But those learners for whom such rules and procedures seem meaningless have great difficulty recalling them, and cannot use them efficiently to solve problems. They may struggle to make sense of the symbols and instructions – or they may just give up in despair. Either way, they do not achieve any real understanding of the concepts that underlie the routines and methods that they are trained to use.

The main purpose of any model or image is to develop the learners' understanding, so they do not just learn *how* to use a method to solve a problem, but they also understand *why* it works. For example, the image of a number line may help some learners to see a subtraction as finding the 'distance' between two numbers.

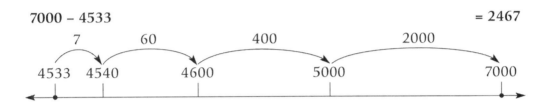

7000 – 4533 = **2467**

This approach may make much better sense than a standard algorithm –

Nought take away three, I can't, borrow one, I can't, borrow one, I can't, borrow one, cross out the seven and put six, make ten in the next column, cross out the ten and make nine, make ten in the next column, cross out the ten and make nine... and so on.

$$7000 \atop 4533$$

$$\begin{matrix} & 6\ 9\ 9 \\ & 7\ 0\ 0\ 0 \\ & 4\ 5\ 3\ 3 \\ \hline & 2\ 4\ 6\ 7 \end{matrix}$$

The number line offers far more than this sequential set of 'rules' for getting the right answer. The picture itself – whether printed, drawn, seen on screen, or just imagined – carries within it an explanation of why the method works. In this way, mathematical ideas from the simplest to the most complex can be made manifest, and so become meaningful and memorable to all our learners – not just to those who struggle to make sense of the printed text.

But the number line, like any other 'model to think with', could be used as just another routine, to be learnt by rote and followed blindly without any understanding of the meaning of each step. Used like this it will be no more helpful, and it will be considerably less tidy, than a numerical algorithm. This book, and the accompanying CD, offer a range of models and images that may be useful, particularly for learners who think more easily in pictures than in words and symbols. By themselves, however, learnt as yet more methods and routines, these models will be useless. If some learners can, and if they really must, learn and recall mathematics without understanding then they will do better to acquire the numerical and symbolic routines. These are generally shorter, neater, and easier to memorise and apply than the pictures and models exemplified in this book. For visual and kinaesthetic thinkers, however, this is not an option. They must understand the mathematics that they are taught. Otherwise they may perhaps learn – but they will almost inevitably forget.

d) Using Symbols and Understanding Diagrams

Our single most important function as maths teachers is to develop our learners' understanding of mathematics. Using mathematical language, manipulating numbers and symbols, applying mathematics to solve problems – all this comes into it, of course. But the basis, the rock on which mathematics education is built, is understanding.

Unfortunately, it is terribly easy to teach learners how to manipulate symbols without understanding. Any teacher with a little determination can teach *how* to add fractions, or *how* to find the area of a circle, or whatever. Learners can learn to get 'right answers' using symbols and the rules for combining them with little understanding of what they mean. Those who can manipulate symbols quickly and efficiently are often thought to be working at a 'higher level' than those who use diagrams or equipment to work through a problem, making sense of each step on the way. A learner who writes

$$\frac{2}{3} + \frac{1}{2} = \frac{2}{3} \times 2 + \frac{1}{2} \times 3 = \frac{4}{6} + \frac{3}{6} = \frac{7}{6} = 1\frac{1}{6}$$

may be rated much more highly that one who uses a more meaningful graphical approach,

But a learner who just goes through the steps, and cannot explain *why* $2/3$ is equal to $4/6$, and $4/6 + 3/6$ is equal to $7/6$ which is equal to $1\,1/6$, is not working at a higher level than a learner who can use, understand and explain the diagrams. These lead, not just to the 'right answer', but to an explanation – a sort of proof that $2/3 + 1/2$ really does equal $11/6$. This involves much more mathematics than any rote learning of meaningless symbolic manipulation. Written numbers and symbols are valuable, and indeed essential, tools for mathematics, but we must always ensure that they are used to express, support and communicate mathematical understanding, not to take its place.

e) Activities and Images – Using the CD

The CD which accompanies this book offers a range of resources, including twenty-odd dynamic PowerPoint presentations showing how models and images may be used to help learners to develop their understanding of key mathematical concepts. You will need the 2003 or later version of PowerPoint to see these. It is important that teachers follow the instructions carefully, clicking the mouse only when there is a small circle in the bottom right-hand corner of the screen. Clicking too soon will cause the program to move on to the next screen, often skipping the animations which are key to the concepts being presented. Pausing provides an opportunity for learners to discuss what is going on and to visualise the movement of the models before they watch the animations on the screen. Teachers will need to play through the presentations that they are going to use in advance so that they can identify the points where they can most usefully pause for comments, visualisation and discussion.

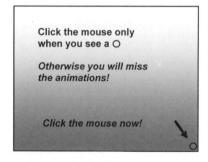

Click the mouse only when you see a O

Otherwise you will miss the animations!

Click the mouse now!

But it should always be remembered that there is not just one model that will work for every learner – there are many possibilities. The chapters that follow, and the accompanying CD, offer a range of suggestions which relate to a variety of topics at different levels, but teachers may well have others that work better in their classrooms. The ideas put forward here are intended primarily as illustrations of an approach – an approach that seeks out *models to think with* that can help learners to develop their understanding. Some of these ideas may be useful for particular learners, but they are only a start. Teachers – and the learners themselves – need to be constantly alert, on the lookout for images and models that will represent and explicate specific concepts. You can start with practically any resource or activity, and see how it could be adapted for visual and kinaesthetic learners. It is the approach that matters, not the details of particular activities or materials. Making mathematical concepts manifest with pictures and models will help all learners – even those who could, if it were really demanded of them, learn and remember routines for getting 'right answers'.

Further Reading and Resources

Paul Black and Dylan Wiliam, 1998: *Inside the Black Box*. King's College, London. Available at http://weaeducation.typepad.co.uk/files/blackbox-1.pdf or at http://www.measuredprogress. org/documents/10157/15653/InsideBlackBox.pdf.

This paper has become a classic, inspiring teachers, schools and governments across the world to re-think assessment strategies and practices. It is worth going back to the original to read the clear and accessible exposition of the arguments and evidence on which the changes have been based.

Jo Boaler, 2010: *The Elephant in the Classroom*. Souvenir Press.
In this very readable book Jo Boaler offers a wealth of sound, practical suggestions, based on a secure and well-researched theoretical structure.

Steve Chinn, 2004: *The Trouble with Maths*. Routledge Falmer.
Steve Chinn, 2012: *More Trouble with Maths*. Routledge Falmer.
In these two books Steve Chinn provides straightforward, applicable advice for teachers working with learners who have a range of difficulties with mathematics.

CHAPTER 2

The Concept of Number

> ## Some key concepts
>
> - A number represents a whole, not just a position in a sequence.
>
> - We can see (*not count*) up to four of any object.
>
> - We can see (*not count*) numbers up to ten with our fingers.
>
> - We can see (*not count*) numbers up to a hundred on the Slavonic abacus.
>
> - We can see (*not count*) complements to a hundred on the Slavonic abacus.

a) Counting and Seeing

When numbers are written on paper or shown on a calculator or a computer screen they are represented by a set of abstract symbols, which to many children are mere squiggles. Children train long and hard to learn which squiggle to associate with which sound – *1* with *one*, *2* with *two*, and so on. They recite the sounds in turn, as they learn to count a group of objects. But the outcome of all this counting and sequential recitation may be to build up an understanding of each number as *a collection of ones*, rather than as a concept in its own right. *Five*, for example, is given meaning and existence primarily as *the number that comes after four*. There is no real understanding of the fiveness of five. Rather, it is seen as the result of *one add one add one add one add one*.

This focus on numbers as a sequence has perhaps been forced on us in the school curriculum by our reliance on print, but it leads to a confusion between the *cardinal* and the *ordinal* aspects of numbers. The NCETM Mathemapedia explains that *A cardinal number arises from counting* – for example, *three* attempts; *eight* books – while *an ordinal number arises from putting things in order* – for example, the *third* attempt; the *eighth* book (see *Further Reading and Resources* below). But defining a cardinal number as that which *arises from counting* is confusing, because the process of counting itself is 'ordinal' in nature. When we count, we recite the number words in order. The cardinal number tells us how many there are in the set – *How many attempts did he make? How many books are on the shelf?* If we always use counting to think about this sort of problem then we will always introduce an ordinal element to our understanding of cardinal numbers.

But we can think about the answer to the question *How many?* in different ways which will encourage a more holistic approach. For some children – and particularly for visual and kinaesthetic learners – thinking of each number as a whole rather than as a collection of units may be much more meaningful.

Most people can scan up to four objects, and see at a glance how many there are, without counting (Butterworth, 1999: 304). This ability to *subitise*, as it is called, lies at the heart of the holistic approach to Number. We can see a collection of four dots, or fingers, or objects, and know that there are four, with no need to go through the sequential process of counting *one, two, three, four*. Some arrangements are easier to see than others, but we can learn to recognise the number of objects in any group of up to four.

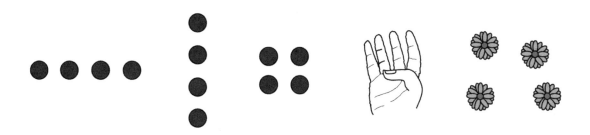

So we can understand *four* not as *one add one add one add one*, but as an image of four objects. Similarly for *one, two* or *three*, we can see the whole, not just the sequence of parts.

So much for numbers up to *four*. But this is a bit limited. How can we go further? The first and most readily available resource is literally to hand. We can learn to see (*see*, not count) up to four fingers on one hand.

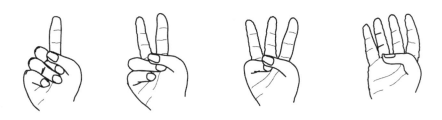

But because it is a coherent whole, we can also see the whole hand, and we can learn that this is a representation of *five* – although other, more random representations of five are much harder to just 'see'. They may have to be counted.

   is easier to see (*not count*) than

So now we have the numbers *one* to *five*, each able to be represented by the digits on one hand.

But, of course, we have two hands.

So, just as we can learn to see (*not count*) that this pattern of fingers is *three*:

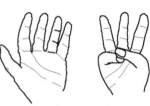

so, in the same way, we can learn to see (*not count*) that this pattern is *eight*:

In this way the numbers one to ten can be represented as patterns of fingers on a pair of hands. This approach helps to establish the concept of each number as a whole, rather than as a part of a sequence. It also offers concrete, rather than symbolic, images of numbers. And finally, the representation of each number involves physical movement. So children can develop an understanding of Number that is based on aural, visual and kinaesthetic images. How much more powerful than any merely symbolic representation!

In the Classroom – *See and Say*

To start with, the teacher can hold up a number of fingers, and call out the total (including, sometimes, *nought* or *zero*). The children copy the teacher.

Then the teacher calls a number up to ten and the children show this on their fingers, or the teacher shows the number and the children call it.

When they are confident, one child can take the teacher's place showing or calling numbers to which the other children respond.

Parents and carers may be encouraged to play this game with individual children for a few minutes each day after school.

But … we have only five digits on each hand. Ten altogether. How can we go beyond 'ten' without symbols? This is where the abacus – some types of abacus – comes in.

b) The Slavonic Abacus

The majority of abaci that are readily available in the UK lead naturally to a 'counting' approach to Number. There are typically five or ten rows of ten beads, with each row painted a different colour – ten red beads, then ten blue, then ten yellow, and so on. Nothing about the row of ten red beads helps us to see (*not count*) numbers up to ten. Given a row of nine identical beads to look at, for example, we have no choice but to count them to discover how many there are:

 cannot be seen *without counting*.

But there are other types of abacus, and some support the *seeing* rather than the *counting* approach to number. One of these is the Slavonic abacus. Slavonic abaci are much more common in other parts of Europe than in the UK or the USA, but they are well worth finding, or making.

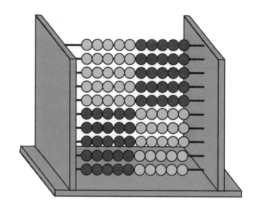

The Slavonic abacus has the usual ten rows of ten beads, but these are coloured in only two, or at the most four, colours, in such a way that each row and each column is made up of five beads of one colour and five of another (Grauberg, 1998: 18–19).

One row of beads on the Slavonic abacus (or a separate stick with ten beads or cubes threaded onto it) allows us to represent numbers up to ten. These are shown in the same way as on a pair of hands, so work on the first row of beads follows naturally from simple finger pattern arithmetic. As with the finger patterns, the emphasis is always on *seeing* whole numbers at a glance, not on counting them one by one.

We can see (*not count*) the numbers *one* to *four* in the usual way.

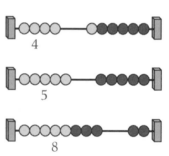

But now we can also see (*not count*) *five* beads, because they are distinguished by their colour from the rest of the row.

And we can learn to see (*not count*) *eight* as a pattern, with five beads of one colour and three of the other.

This approach to whole numbers up to 10 has the great strength that every number is seen with its complement to 10, so each number becomes deeply associated with its complement. The *two* that goes with *eight*, for example, becomes an inbuilt aspect of the concept of the number *eight*.

But the way in which the beads on the Slavonic abacus are coloured allows us to go further, and to see numbers up to 100, with their complements to 100. For example, we can see that this abacus shows *seventy-two* beads – that is, seven whole rows, plus two single beads. We can also see that there are *twenty-eight* beads – two whole rows, plus eight single beads – left over to make the full complement of a hundred.

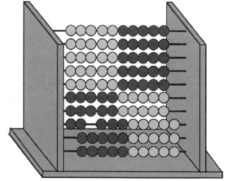

So the Slavonic abacus offers learners a way to understand each number up to a hundred, not as a point in a recited sequence, but rather as a whole that is seen, not counted. This whole may then be associated with the relevant symbol – 6 with a row of six beads, for example, or *40* with four rows of ten. Place value and its use in the representation of multi-digit numbers are discussed in more detail in Chapter 4, *Place Value and*

Decimals, but the abacus provides a visual and kinaesthetic experience which will give learners a thorough grasp of the concept of Number. Their understanding of the symbols which are used to represent numbers will then be based on a meaningful, and therefore memorable, concept.

In the Classroom – *Numbers and their Complements*

Using a large Slavonic abacus or a single ten-bead stick, the teacher shows a one-digit number on the top row. The learners call the number, and then they call its complement to ten. They may also show first the number, then its complement, on their fingers.

In the same way, the teacher uses the whole abacus to show a two-digit number, being careful to move all the rows of *ten* in one movement, followed by the *one* beads. So to show the number *forty-six*, for example, the teacher moves the top four rows of the abacus across, and the learners call 'forty…'.

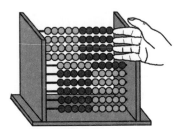

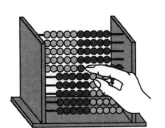

Then the teacher moves six beads in the fifth row across, and the learners call '…six'.

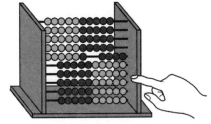

Now the teacher points to the remaining beads, and the learners say, 'and fifty-four make a hundred'.

If a Slavonic abacus is unavailable then blocks of interlocking cubes, or a printed grid (see Resource Sheet 2-1) with a coloured transparent plastic sheet cut to mask dots to the right and below the number being shown, may be used instead to convey the same ideas. Alternatively, a free electronic Slavonic abacus may be downloaded from the internet (see *Further Reading and Resources*, below).

However, neither the static grid or model nor the electronic abacus offer the same kinaesthetic experience as an actual Slavonic abacus made of beads that can be manipulated by the teacher and the learners. You are very strongly encouraged to obtain at least one real abacus, so that your learners can feel the beads moving under their fingers. These abaci can be bought (see *Further Reading and Resources*, below), but they are quite expensive. The best solution may be to find an old conventional 100-bead abacus and two cans of spray paint in contrasting colours, put on an apron, and paint it yourself!

The Concept of Number – Teaching Points

- Learners' understanding of Number is key to their mathematical development.

- Numbers may be **counted** in a sequence or **seen** as wholes.

- Learners spend a lot of time counting, but less attention may be paid to seeing the whole.

- Kinaesthetic and visual representations of numbers will help all learners to understand numbers as wholes.

- Representing whole numbers up to 10 on a pair of hands enables learners to see and feel the mathematical structure of numbers.

- One- and two-digit numbers may be represented on a Slavonic abacus.

- Learners can see the complements to 10 or 100 of numbers represented on the Slavonic abacus.

- Such representations enable learners to see, *not count*, a number of objects. This is called *subitising*.

Resources on the CD

Resource Sheet

RS 2-1 *Slavonic Abacus Grids*

Further Reading and Resources

Brian Butterworth, 1999: *The Mathematical Brain*. London: Macmillan.
This is the seminal work on subitisation – the ability to see a number of objects, without counting.

Eva Grauberg, 1998: *Elementary Mathematics and Language Difficulties*. London: Whurr Publishers.
Eva Grauberg's book provides an excellent background discussion of the Slavonic abacus and many of its uses.

NCETM Mathemapedia: https://www.ncetm.org.uk/mathemapedia/
The NCETM Mathemapedia is a valuable first port of call for a clear explanation of the mathematical terms and concepts that teachers and learners are likely to meet.

You can download a free electronic **Slavonic abacus** from the Xavier website at the University of Bangor (go to http://www.xavier-educational-software.co.uk/index.shtml, and try all the options for 'Slavonic Abacus'). But it is most important that your learners are able to see and handle a real one – please don't restrict them to the virtual version!

A fairly large classroom abacus may be bought from the Xavier website, or from Tomoe Soroban (http://www.soroban.com/index_eng.html). Otherwise, find an old, conventional 100-bead abacus and re-paint it yourself.

A static electronic Slavonic abacus for work on complements to 100 can be downloaded from the Barking and Dagenham College Content Workshop (http://vle.barkingdagenhamcollege. ac.uk/cw_testbed/resources/junior/maths/abacus/abacus_disk/start.htm).

Models for Multiplication and Division

Some key concepts

- Multiplication may be understood using an area model.

- Single-digit multiplication may be modelled on the Slavonic abacus.

- An image of a large rectangle divided into smaller rectangles provides an area model for long multiplication.

- A different 'picture in the mind', modelling the process of repeated subtraction, is needed for long division.

---

a) Multiplication Arrays – 'Seeing' up to Four Fours

To visual and kinaesthetic thinkers, arithmetic can seem very daunting. There are so many numbers. Masses of those wretched squiggles, and endless rules for putting them together. To learners who think more easily in pictures than in words and symbols neither the squiggles nor the rules will make much sense. So the challenge for the teacher is to find ways to present the important concepts, supporting them with visual and kinaesthetic 'pictures in the mind' which the learners can use as tools to think with.

Multiplying two numbers can be thought of as finding the area of a rectangle. Learners can learn to recognise arrays of up to four by four, and associate them with their totals. So, for example, they can see the array

○ ○ ○
○ ○ ○

as two rows of three, and they can learn to recognise this as *six*.

Arrays like this may be printed onto cards, to be handled by learners until they become very familiar. These cards do not have a 'right way up' – so for example, it is clear that:

 and are both equally *six*. The concept of commutativity – that two threes are the same as three twos – becomes established as a fact relating to the patterns of dots, not to the inter-changeability of squiggles.

Similarly, the squareness of square numbers becomes self evident –

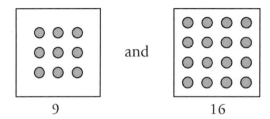

for example, are square numbers because they are square, not just because they are squiggles multiplied by themselves.

Just as learners can learn to see, *not count*, a row or column of up to four beads, so they can learn to see, *not count*, an array of up to four by four beads. This will give them the 'pictures in the mind' they need to enable them to visualise, and so recall, the multiplication facts up to 4×4. These need to be established first, before learners go on to work with multiplication facts involving larger numbers, 5 and above.

In the Classroom – *Dotty Arrays*

A set of posters showing each of the arrays from one by two to four by four can be found on the CD (Poster 3-1 *Dotty Arrays: Array Cards – Teacher's Set*). Working with the whole class, the teacher holds up the arrays one at a time in random order and the learners call both the total product and its two factors. Resource Sheet 3-1 can be used to prepare sets of array cards for individual learners. When they are confident, learners can work in pairs to build up speed so they can instantly recognise, for example, the three by four array as *twelve* whatever its orientation – three by four, four by three, or on a slant.

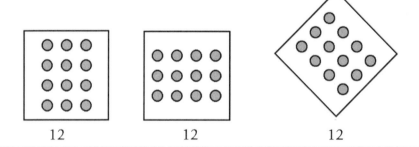

PowerPoint

PowerPoint 3-1, *Dotty Arrays*, allows learners to practise recognising arrays up to four by four without having to count the number of dots.

Theme: Making Links – Arrays and Factors

Blocks of interlocking cubes can also be used to represent each array. These have the advantage that they can be split up and re-combined, to demonstrate the process of factorisation – so *four threes*, for example, can be broken up and reassembled into *two sixes*.

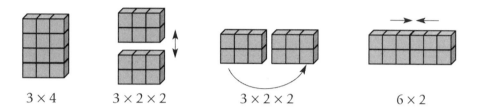

| 3×4 | $3 \times 2 \times 2$ | $3 \times 2 \times 2$ | 6×2 |

This can help learners to appreciate, not just the 'facts' of the multiplication tables, but their underlying structure and inter-relationships.

b) Multiplying up to Ten by Ten

Just as it is hard to see, *not count*, a row or column of seven or eight identical beads, so it is hard to see, *not count*, an array involving a pair of numbers over five, such as *seven eights*. But here again, the Slavonic abacus can provide the 'picture in the mind' that we need.

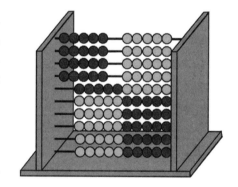

First, learners must learn to recognise the products in the five times table. These may be modelled using the beads on one side of the Slavonic abacus. *So four fives*, for example, may be represented as four rows of five beads.

These four rows are then grouped into pairs, to give *two tens*.

Alternatively, this relationship can be modelled with interlocking cubes. The four rows of five can be broken up into two blocks of two by five, then joined up again to make two rows of ten.

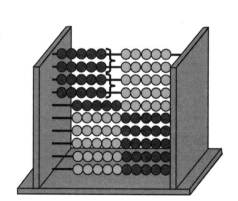

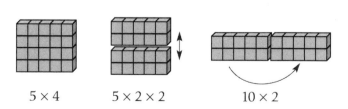

| 5×4 | $5 \times 2 \times 2$ | 10×2 |

In the Classroom – *Multiplying by Five*

Teachers can use the Slavonic abacus to demonstrate multiplication facts for five, such as the relationship between *seven fives* and *three tens plus five*.

Then learners can use interlocking cubes to build a model of the same relationship, and of others in the five times table.

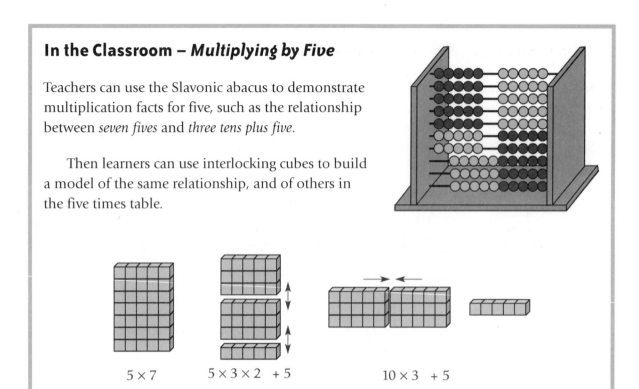

5×7 $5 \times 3 \times 2 + 5$ $10 \times 3 + 5$

Once learners know the products up to ten times five – and understand them as rearrangements of the fives into pairs to make tens – they can go on to multiply higher single digit numbers.

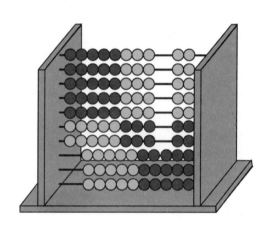

To create a model for the product of *seven* and *eight*, for example, an array of seven rows of eight must be set up on the abacus. Learners should be able to set this array in one movement, selecting the seven rows of eight beads at a glance, without counting.

The array on the Slavonic abacus splits into four rectangles, identified by their colours. On the left are two rectangles, comprising seven rows of five – five in one colour, and two in the other. On the right are three *columns* of five in one colour, plus a three by two rectangle. So altogether we have ten fives – seven rows of five plus three columns of five – plus six, giving a total of fifty-six.

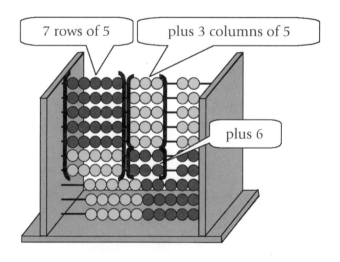

7 rows of 5   plus 3 columns of 5   plus 6

Here again a printed grid, this time with an L-shaped shield to mark off the product being calculated, may be used if no Slavonic abacus is available (see Resource Sheet 2-1). So to calculate the product of *nine* and *seven*, for example, we shield off an array of nine rows of seven.

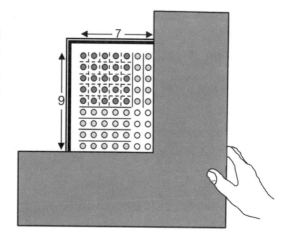

This gives nine rows of five on the left, plus two columns of five on the right, plus eight. So we have eleven fives plus eight, or fifty-five plus eight, which is sixty-three.

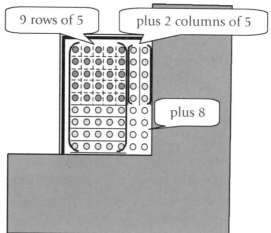

9 rows of 5

plus 2 columns of 5

plus 8

In the Classroom – *Practising the Multiplication Tables*

Teachers can set up arrays on the Slavonic abacus for the products of single digits, and learners can first say what product is being represented and then give the total. When they are confident, learners can practise using the abacus or the grid to find products of pairs of single digits by themselves. With time, they will develop a mental image of the arrays on a Slavonic abacus which they can recall and use to calculate the elusive 'number facts' of the multiplication tables.

This approach to single-digit multiplication may well seem tedious and long-winded to those learners who are able simply to learn the multiplication tables off by heart. But for learners for whom these chanted tables are just gobbledegook –

Grue chups are glonk

Grue sleps are fruggle

and so on, a 'picture in the mind' may be much more meaningful. For visual and kinaesthetic learners, learning without understanding is not an option – they will just forget. So in the long run, although it takes more effort to 'see' the rows and columns of five and the rectangle in the bottom right corner, and to put all the rows and columns together to find the product, a mental image of the Slavonic abacus is much easier to recall when it is needed.

But here again, if the use of the Slavonic abacus is taught as just another 'method', a series of steps to be followed blindly in order to find a 'right answer', it will not help at all. The abacus does not simply state that 'seven eights are fifty-six': it offers a visible representation of the number fifty-six as the product of seven and eight. If learners are to remember this method, and to use it effectively, then they must understand the *why*, not just know the *how*.

In the Classroom – *Handy Multiplication*

Another method for finding the harder multiplication facts from the six, seven, eight and nine times tables is also worth mentioning. It requires learners to memorise a routine – but the routine is something to do, rather than something to say, so it may be helpful for kinaesthetic learners who can remember movements more easily than words.

The thumb and fingers of each hand are first labelled with the numbers 6 to 10. (Learners – and teachers – can wear a pair of plastic gloves if they need to keep their fingers clean!)

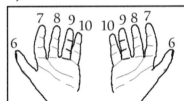

Then the tips of the two fingers whose numbers are to be multiplied are brought together so they are just touching. For example, to multiply 7 by 8 the tip of the forefinger (labelled 7) must just touch the tip of the middle finger (labelled 8) to form a link. Now the two touching fingers, and all the fingers (and the thumbs) above them, are counted, giving 2 on one hand and 3 on the other – or 5 altogether. This is the number of *tens* in the total product.

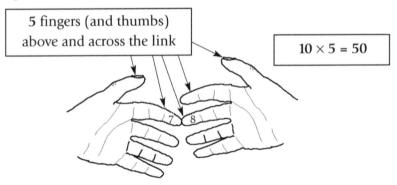

5 fingers (and thumbs) above and across the link

$10 \times 5 = 50$

Next we look at the fingers below the link – the 'danglies'. There are 3 on one hand and 2 on the other. These two numbers are multiplied together, and the product, 6, is added to the *5 tens* we already have.

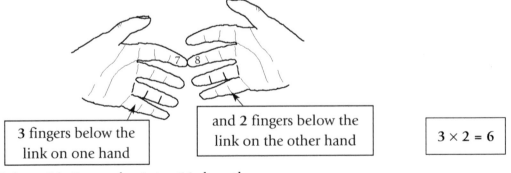

3 fingers below the link on one hand

and 2 fingers below the link on the other hand

$3 \times 2 = 6$

So 7 times 8 is *5 tens, plus 6* – or 56 altogether.

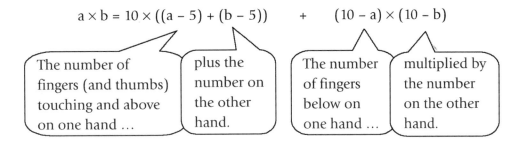

If you want to see how *Handy Multiplication* works then the formula you need is:

$$a \times b = 10 \times ((a - 5) + (b - 5)) \quad + \quad (10 - a) \times (10 - b)$$

The number of fingers (and thumbs) touching and above on one hand …

plus the number on the other hand.

The number of fingers below on one hand …

multiplied by the number on the other hand.

It is unlikely that many learners will be able to follow this algebra – but for some, the movements can be memorised and recalled much more easily than the recited chants of the multiplication tables.

c) Multi-digit Multiplication – the Area Model

The 'rules' for long multiplication are amongst the most confusing and incomprehensible that learners have to contend with.

Multiply the end underneath number by each of the top numbers in turn, carrying the left-hand digit whenever the answer is more than nine. Then put a nought on the end of the next line, and multiply the next underneath number by each of the top numbers. Then if there is another underneath number you put two noughts on the next line, and … and so on. Oh – and you work the other way round from the way you read: right to left, not left to right.

Just remembering when and where to put in the noughts is hard! Doing each of the computations in turn, in the right order, without ever losing one's place – that is well nigh impossible for many learners.

Fortunately, an alternative approach using an 'area' model for multi-digit multiplication has become much better established in recent years. For example, to calculate *27 × 14*, the figures are shown as the lengths of the sides of a rectangle. Then the rectangle is divided up into six parts, and the area of each part is found separately. Finally these are added together to find the area of the whole rectangle.

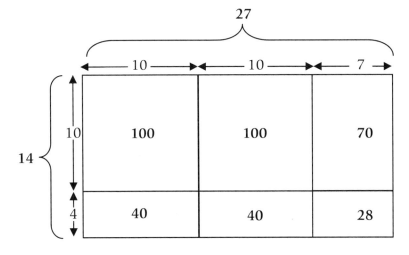

The area model of multiplication has a number

$$100 + 100 + 70 + 40 + 40 + 28 = 378$$

of advantages over the standard written algorithm. The different parts of the computation are tied directly to different parts of the rectangle, so it is easier to keep track of them. The most significant numbers (in the example above, the *tens* values from the *27* and the *14*) are multiplied first – while in the standard written algorithm, all the attention is focused first on the relatively insignificant *7* and *4*. But above all, the area model is meaningful. It allows learners to see *why* the *2* in the *27* multiplied by the *1* in the *14* gives *200*, not *2*.

But here again, to make it worth while learners must understand what the model represents. Without that understanding the area model is no more memorable, and may be considerably less tidy and concise, than the conventional numerical algorithm.

PowerPoint

PowerPoint 3-2, *Area Model for Multiplication*, shows how the different parts of a 2-digit by 2-digit multiplication fit together.

---

d) Division

Division is a tricky concept for all learners – but particularly for visual and kinaesthetic thinkers. Mathematically speaking, division is the inverse of multiplication – so if *27 × 14 = 378*, for example, then *378 ÷ 14 = 27*. Using an area model for multiplication, we can say *The area of a 27 by 14 rectangle is 378*. This can be rephrased as a division to give *A rectangle with an area of 378 and one side of length 14 must have another side of length 27*.

The area model works well for multiplication. If I know the lengths of its two sides then I can build up a visual image of the whole rectangle. I can *imagine* the rectangle, even if I have not yet started to split it up into its smaller rectangles in order to work out its area.

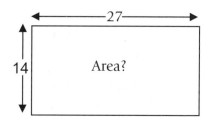

But if all I know are the area and the length of one side, it is much harder to visualise the rectangle. I do not know what shape it is.

Is it this shape?   Or this shape?   Or.... ?

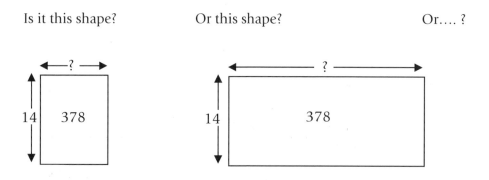

Steve Chinn recommends a 'repeated subtraction' approach to division (Chinn, 2004: 23). This does not lend itself well to the area-based image of a rectangle. Rather, it needs a more nebulous, undefined shape to represent the total product which is to be divided. A pile of counters that can be split up into a number of smaller heaps may offer a more useful 'picture in the mind' for division.

For example, 378 ÷ 14 may be thought of as 'How many 14s are there in 378?' To model this, we need to imagine a pile of 378 counters, to be sorted into heaps of 14.

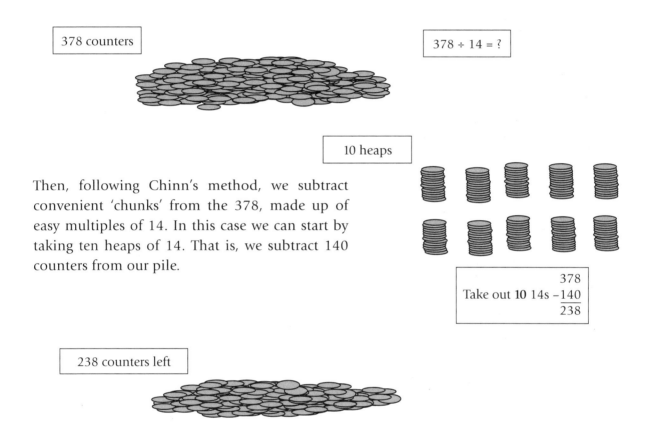

378 counters

378 ÷ 14 = ?

10 heaps

Then, following Chinn's method, we subtract convenient 'chunks' from the 378, made up of easy multiples of 14. In this case we can start by taking ten heaps of 14. That is, we subtract 140 counters from our pile.

$$\begin{array}{r} 378 \\ \text{Take out } \mathbf{10}\ 14\text{s} -140 \\ \hline 238 \end{array}$$

238 counters left

This reduces our pile a bit, but we still have 238 counters left. We can take out another ten heaps, giving us 20 heaps so far.

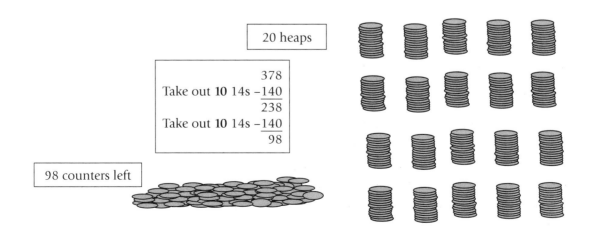

20 heaps

$$\begin{array}{r} 378 \\ \text{Take out } \mathbf{10}\ 14\text{s} -140 \\ \hline 238 \\ \text{Take out } \mathbf{10}\ 14\text{s} -140 \\ \hline 98 \end{array}$$

98 counters left

Now we are left with 98 counters. Not enough for another ten heaps, but we can manage five more. That will remove another 70 counters from the pile, and give us 25 heaps.

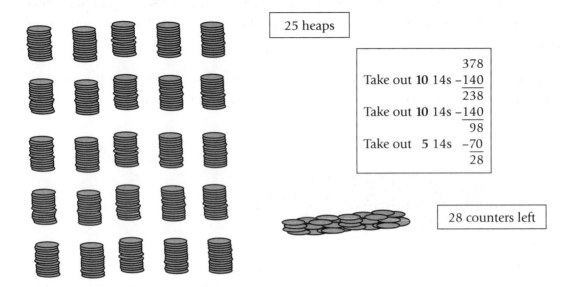

25 heaps

```
                        378
Take out 10 14s  −140
                        238
Take out 10 14s  −140
                         98
Take out  5 14s   −70
                         28
```

28 counters left

Now we have twenty-five heaps of 14 counters, and there are 28 left in the pile. That is just enough for 2 more heaps.

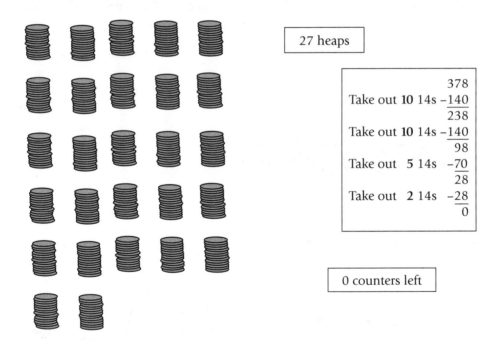

27 heaps

```
                        378
Take out 10 14s  −140
                        238
Take out 10 14s  −140
                         98
Take out  5 14s   −70
                         28
Take out  2 14s   −28
                          0
```

0 counters left

So now we have divided all of our 378 counters into heaps of 14, giving us 10 + 10 + 5 + 2, or 27, heaps all together.

This example serves to illustrate Chinn's 'repeated subtraction' approach to division. Some learners may be able to take out larger numbers of counters in one go, for example by subtracting 20 piles of 14, or 280 counters, at the first step. Others might have to go more slowly, removing fewer counters at a time from the pile. The important point is to ensure that learners have a 'picture in the mind' to help them to understand what is happening at each step as they divide the pile of 378 counters into heaps of 14.

PowerPoint

PowerPoint 3-3, *Two Models for Division*, shows how division may be viewed either as *How many?* or as *Share between*. These two models give rise to different 'pictures in the mind', but they lead to the same set of figures and calculations.

Those learners who do eventually go on to use the conventional algorithm for long division will find that the model still holds. To divide 8802 by 27, for example, we start by finding that there are **300** 27s ('300 piles of 27', or 8100) in 8802, with 702 left. In the 702 there are **20** 27s (540), with 162 left. The remaining 162 gives us another **6** 27s, so we have a total of 300 + 20 + 6, or **326** 27s in 8802.

$$
\begin{array}{r}
326 \\
27\overline{)8802} \\
8100 \\
\hline
702 \\
540 \\
\hline
162 \\
162 \\
\hline
0
\end{array}
$$

Models for Multiplication and Division – Teaching Points

- Arithmetic can be very daunting for visual and kinaesthetic thinkers.

- The multiplication of two numbers is more meaningful if it is thought of as finding the area of a rectangle.

- For single-digit multiplication, arrays and the Slavonic abacus offer useful models.

- Long multiplication can be understood using an area model.

- Division requires a different model to multiplication.

- The conventional algorithm for long division is based on repeated subtraction. This may be adapted using a 'picture in the mind', such as a pile of counters being distributed into equal-sized heaps.

Resources on the CD

Mathematical PowerPoints

    PP 3-1 *Dotty Arrays*

    PP 3-2 *Area Model for Multiplication*

    PP 3-3 *Two Models for Division*

Resource Sheet

    RS 3-1 *Array Cards*

Posters

P 3-1 *Dotty Arrays: Array Cards – Teacher's Set*

P 3-2 *Slavonic Multiplication*

P 3-3 *Handy Multiplication*

Further Reading and Resources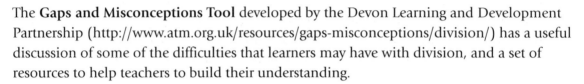

The **Gaps and Misconceptions Tool** developed by the Devon Learning and Development Partnership (http://www.atm.org.uk/resources/gaps-misconceptions/division/) has a useful discussion of some of the difficulties that learners may have with division, and a set of resources to help teachers to build their understanding.

Steve Chinn, 2004: *The Trouble with Maths*. Routledge Falmer.

Straightforward, applicable advice for teachers working with learners who have a range of difficulties with mathematics.

CHAPTER 4

Place Value and Decimals

> **Some key concepts**
>
> - We use the position of a digit in a multi-digit number to show its place value.
>
> - Place value represents the *relative scale* of each digit in a multi-digit number.
>
> - The cycle *cubes → sticks → slabs → cubes* gives us a 'picture in the mind' of place value at any position in the system.
>
> - A *1 000* cube is the same shape as a *1* cube or a *1 000 000* cube. It is just on a different scale.
>
> - The model for *4.378* is the same as the model for *4 378*. Again, it is just on a different scale.
>
> - When a number is multiplied by 10, the digits move one position to the left. The decimal point stays put.

a) Whole Number Place Value

Place value in our number system tells us the size of a number. Because we use a decimal system, place value gives us the size in powers of ten – *1s, 10s, 100s, 1000s* and so on. Any number, no matter how big, is broken up into its constituent powers of ten – so *three hundred and seventy-six*, for example, is exactly what it says: three hundreds, seven tens, and six ones.

The key to understanding place value is *scale*. The calculation *400 + 200*, for example, works in the same way as the calculation *4 + 2*. The numbers are similar – they are just on a bigger *scale*. *40* is ten times as much as *4*, and *400* is ten times as much as *40*, and so on. This idea lies at the heart of our representation of whole numbers. Place value is just a symbolic representation of the powers of ten, so it can be visualised as a representation of *scale*. Place value equipment – Diennes blocks and other base 10 materials – usually represent *1* as a single unit cube, *10* as ten cubes in a stick, *100* as ten sticks in a slab, and *1000* as a ten slabs in a bigger cube.

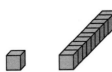
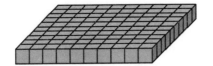
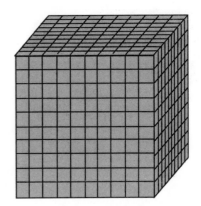
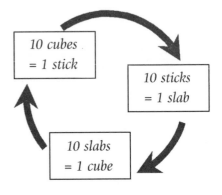

And then the cycle starts again. We can imagine, even if we cannot actually represent, ten *1 000* cubes that make up a *10 000* stick, ten *10 000* sticks in a *100 000* slab, and ten *100 000* slabs in a *1 000 000* cube. If the single unit *1* cube has an edge length of one centimetre then the *1 000* cube will be ten centimetres cubed, while the *1 000 000* cube will be a whopping metre cubed. These are much too big to make with ordinary base 10 materials, although a good model of a cubic metre may be made with twelve garden canes cut to size and fastened together with stiff wire at the corners. (The wire needs to be stiff because otherwise the whole frame will lean over and will not look cubic at all!) But the cycle, from cubes to sticks to slabs to cubes, goes on and on. It gives us a 'picture in the mind' of whole numbers getting infinitely large, but always in a precise, controlled pattern.

10 cubes = 1 stick

10 sticks = 1 slab

10 slabs = 1 cube

PowerPoint

PowerPoints 4-1 to 4-3, *Whole Number Place Value 1, 2 and 3*, present a dynamic image of the *cubes → sticks → slabs → cubes* cycle. With each complete loop of the cycle a new cube is created, composed of a thousand of the previous cubes. Then the cycle starts again.

It is a bit awkward, though, that the *1*, the *10* and the *100* are completely different shapes. It may be difficult to see how for instance,

4 + 2　　=　　6

can work in the same way as

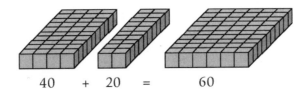

40　+　20　=　　60

The *1* cubes are there, at the ends of the *10* sticks – but the cubes and sticks are different shapes, so they cannot fit together in the same way.

On the other hand, making *1* and *10* the same shape – so they are both cubes, for instance, where the *10* cube has ten times the volume of the *1* cube – does not work either. It is not obvious that

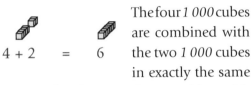

if this is *1*: ▢ then this is *10*: ▢

even though the edge of the *10* cube is $\sqrt[3]{10}$ times as long as the *1* cube, so its volume has been multiplied by 10. We cannot see the ten *1*s in the *10* here, as we can see the ten *1* cubes in a *10* stick.

This being the case, children who think more easily in pictures than in words and numbers may actually find it easier to see the connection between, say, *4* and *4 000*, than between *4* and *40* or *400*. Using conventional base 10 materials, *4* is represented by four *1* cubes, and *4 000* is represented by four *1 000* cubes. The 'model to think with' for *4 000 + 2 000* is exactly the same as the model for *4 + 2*. It is just bigger.

The four *1 000* cubes are combined with the two *1 000* cubes in exactly the same way as the four *1* cubes combine with the two *1* cubes. We can see the thousand *1*s in the *1 000*, but we can also see the *1 000* as a whole, so we can think in thousands.

4 + 2   =   6

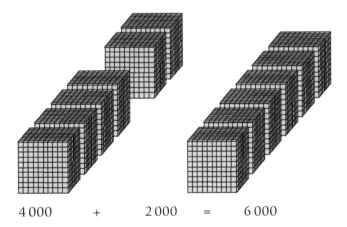

4 000   +   2 000   =   6 000

In the Classroom – *Modelling Whole Numbers*

Learners who have difficulty interpreting printed symbols and numerals are likely to find written work on place value hard to understand and remember. They need something, a model or a mental image, to hang the symbols on to. Teachers can use base 10 equipment or interlocking cubes to model a number with up to four digits.

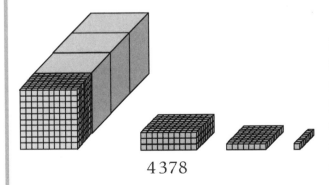

4 378

Sets of base 10 equipment rarely have more than one *1 000* cube, but it is not difficult to make these so that numbers over *2 000* can be modelled. If the *1* cube is a centimetre cube then extra *1 000* cubes, 10 centimetres by 10 centimetres by 10 centimetres, may be made from card or thick paper.

b) Decimal Place Value

The idea that *4 000* is the same shape as *4*, but bigger, suggests a way to think about decimal numbers. If *4 000* is the same as *4*, but a thousand times bigger, then *4.378*, for example, is the same as *4 378*, but a thousand times smaller. There is nothing new to learn about the numbers: we are just 'zooming in', seeing the thousand little thousandth cubes inside each unit cube. The model for the two numbers is the same – but in one case we are working with units, and in the other with thousandths.

Theme: Making Links – Decimal Place Value and Capacity

It may be useful, at this point, to make the connection with capacity. If *1* is represented by a centimetre cube then it has a capacity of a millilitre. In that case, the *1 000* cube has a capacity of a litre. So the model can be seen as representing either *4 378* millilitres or *4.378* litres – it depends how it is viewed.

In the Classroom – *Modelling Decimal Numbers*

The same model will serve equally well to represent a 4-figure whole number, like *4 378*, or a number which is less than *10* but runs to three decimal places, such as *4.378*.

In a decimal number greater than *10*, however, the centimetre cube must represent *1*, so for the decimal part of the number we need *0.1* 'slabs' on the same scale as the whole numbers. These are the slabs one would get by slicing a centimetre cube into ten. Making these may seem more difficult, but in fact thick card, from a shoe box or from the back of a pad of paper, is usually about a millimetre thick – or near enough.

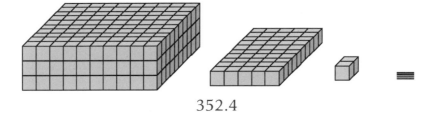

352.4

Centimetre squares can be cut from this card, and ten of these will lie on top of each other to form a cube (of sorts) about a centimetre high. Each of these 1 centimetre by 1 centimetre by 1 millimetre slabs represents *0.1* on the same scale as the centimetre cubes representing *1*.

One of these card centimetre squares may again be cut into ten 'sticks' a millimetre wide, and even into millimetre cubes, to represent the *0.01*s and the *0.001*s, if these are required.

The bits of the number are getting almost too small to see and handle now – but this gets across the idea of the relative sizes of whole numbers and decimals in a very powerful manner. And while it would obviously be absurd to try to slice the tiny millimetre cubed *0.001* cube into *0.0001* slabs one tenth of a millimetre thick, the idea is there. The same cycle as we used for whole numbers, but going in reverse – from cubes to slabs to sticks – can give us the 'picture in the mind' that we need to see decimal numbers getting infinitely small, but still according to a strict, regular pattern.

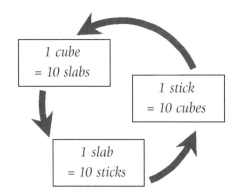

PowerPoint

PowerPoint 4-4, *Decimal Place Value*, shows the reversed cycle, *cubes → slabs → sticks → cubes*, with the models indicating how the place value of each digit is just one-tenth of the previous one.

c) Using Symbols to Represent Whole Number Place Value

We have seen that the key to understanding place value is scale. But the key to understanding the use of numbers and symbols to *represent* place value is *movement*. When *4* is multiplied by 10, so that it becomes *40*, it *moves*. It moves one place to the left.

But the trouble is, it doesn't. Few teachers would ever actually teach a learner that they should 'add a nought' to multiply a whole number by ten – but that, in reality, is what happens. If written symbols are used to represent *4 multiplied by 10* then the teacher may talk about the *4* moving up one place to the left, but to the learner it is obvious that the *4* stays put. The *0* just takes up its position after it.

4
40

Calculators can certainly help here. They do not just 'add a nought' when a whole number is multiplied by 10: they visibly move the number one position to the left. Teachers may hesitate to encourage learners to use a calculator to do something as 'easy' as multiplying a whole number by 10 – but getting the right answer really is not the point here. The calculator offers a 'picture to think with' which will help to combat learners' misconceptions about the function of the '0' in this context.

4

40

400

In the Classroom – *Modelling Place Value*

A chart showing how each written number relates to its model will help to give meaning to the written symbols.

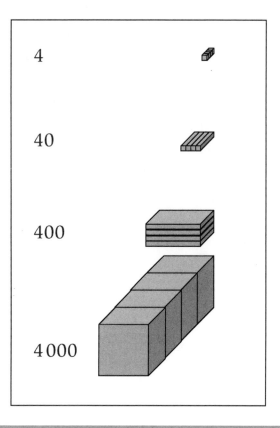

In the Classroom – *Place Value and Position*

Learners can also make a 'folding number', cut out of a sheet of A4 paper, to show how a multi-digit number breaks down into its constituent parts. *376*, for instance, breaks down into *300*, *70* and *6*, while *444* breaks down into *400*, *40* and *4*. See Resource Sheet 4-1, *Folding Number*.

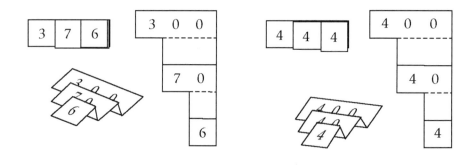

d) Using Symbols to Represent Decimal Place Value

Although it is a valuable tool to help learners to understand what happens when a whole number is multiplied by 10, with decimal numbers the calculator undermines its own good teaching practice. What appears on the screen when 24.69 is multiplied by 10 is 246.9 Most of the digits are in the same place as before: it is the decimal point that appears to have moved, swapping positions with the 6. This image does not convey the key concept of the movement of all the digits up one place to the left. So rather than a calculator, teachers need to use resources and activities that emphasise that the digits move while the decimal point stays put.

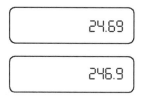

In the Classroom – *The Decimal Slide*

A sliding model which demonstrates the movement of the digits when a decimal number is multiplied or divided by a power of ten can be made out of a sheet of A4 paper. The paper is folded and two windows are cut, with the decimal point between them.

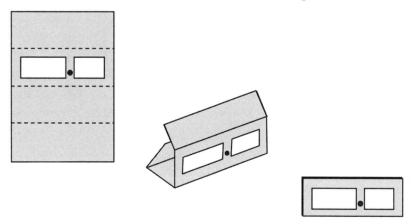

Then a 1- or 2-digit number, followed by some 0s, are written on a strip of paper.

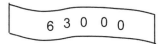

The strip of paper is fed through one end of the folded paper to slide beneath the windows.

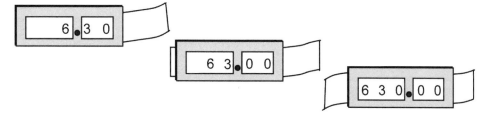

As the strip slides to the left, the number is multiplied by 10: as it slides to the right, it is divided by 10. See Resource Sheets 4.2, *Decimal Slide Holder* and 4.3, *Decimal Slide Number*.

(Continued)

(Continued)

The vital role played by the *0* as a 'place holder' in, say, the number *630* becomes clear with this sliding model. If we did not have the *0* to fill the units column then there would be nothing to distinguish *630* from *63*. Even if the paper strip is too short to show them all, we can imagine a string of *0*s trailing off to the right, ready to slide up as the number on the strip is multiplied by ten again and again. A larger model, and a longer strip, would allow for numbers with more digits – but a model made from a sheet of A4 paper, with two non-zero digits and three zeros, will get the idea across. It will give learners a visual and kinaesthetic 'picture in the mind' of the movement of the digits across the decimal point that they are far more likely to remember than any number of written exercises on static, printed sheets.

In the Classroom – *Learner Numbers*

A row of learners, each holding a card or number fan showing one digit of a 'decimal number', stand on either side of a fixed decimal point drawn on a flip chart. On the command *Multiply by ten* all the learners move up one place; *Divide by a hundred* means they must all move down two places; and so on. Other calculations involving a change to a single digit may also be used – so *subtract ten*, for example, means that the learner currently in the 'tens' position must swap their card for one with a lower value, while *add nought point three* means that the learner two places down must display a higher-value card. This activity helps to focus attention on the position of each digit, and on the way this changes depending on the magnitude of the number being displayed.

All the models and activities that teachers can use to explain whole numbers and decimals, and their multiplication and division by powers of ten, have one driving purpose. They all offer a 'picture in the mind' that the learner can use to make sense of place value. Symbols and rules may mean little in themselves, and are easily forgotten. But once the conventions have meaning, learners are far more likely to recall and use them effectively.

Place Value and Decimals – Teaching Points

- The concept of place value is essential to the representation of both whole and decimal numbers.

- The key to understanding place value is *scale*.

- The relative scale of digits occupying different positions in a multi-digit number may be represented by the cubes → sticks → slabs → cubes cycle.

- The key to the representation of place value is *movement*.

- The movement should be demonstrated, not on static paper, but with a sliding model.

Resources on the CD

Mathematical PowerPoints

> PP 4-1 *Whole Number Place Value 1 – Cubes, Sticks and Slabs*
>
> PP 4-2 *Whole Number Place Value 2 – Modelling Numbers*
>
> PP 4-3 *Whole Number Place Value 3 – Multiplying by 10*
>
> PP 4-4 *Decimal Place Value*

Resource Sheets

> RS 4-1 *Folding Number*
>
> RS 4-2 *Decimal Slide Holder*
>
> RS 4-3 *Decimal Slide Number*

Further Reading and Resources

Number fans may be obtained from http://www.hope-education.co.uk/home. Alternatively, search for 'Number fan' and download a set to print and cut out yourself.

C HAPTER 5

Fractions

Some key concepts

■ Fractions are just bits of things. They have shape and pattern.

■ The numerical representation of a fraction, such as $3/4$, carries many different meanings.

■ The key concept is that *n n^{th}s make a whole one*.

■ To add, subtract or divide fractions we need to make sure that we are working with the same-sized bits. These are what we call *equivalent fractions*.

■ The multiplication of fractions may again be understood with an area model.

■ Diagrams and models can be used to explain and justify, not just to do, calculations. This is the basis of mathematical proof.

a) Symbols and Images

The 'four rules' for the manipulation of fractions are some of the most complicated, confusing, and just plain bizarre that are ever inflicted on children in our schools.

> *To add two fractions, you give them a common denominator by multiplying the top and bottom numbers by the same number and then you add the two top numbers and then you cancel down.*

> *To multiply two fractions you multiply the two top numbers together and the two bottom numbers together and then you cancel down.*

> *To divide one fraction by another you turn them upside down … No, you turn the first one … No, the second one … Well, anyway, you turn one of them upside down and then you multiply. Or is it divide? Divide would make more sense …. Oh, and then you cancel down. When in doubt, always cancel down. You may get a mark.*

No wonder learners – even relatively numerate learners, who can remember the multiplication tables at least some of the time – get confused. For a visual and kinaesthetic thinker the whole thing can be a nightmare.

It need not be. Fractions, after all, are just bits of things. They have shape and pattern. They can be understood spatially. But the numbers can get in the way.

The problem with fractions is that, like so much of mathematics, they are usually represented with symbols. So the universal representation of *three quarters*, for example, is $3/4$, not

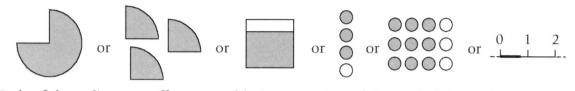

Each of these diagrams offers a possible interpretation of the symbol $3/4$. And like numbers represented on the Slavonic abacus, each one also carries a representation of the complement to the whole one – the 'missing' quarter.

The symbol $3/4$ can have any of the interrelated meanings represented by the diagrams, and many more besides – three out of every four of something; forty-five minutes in an hour; the probability of getting exactly two heads or exactly two tails if I toss a coin three times; three divided by four, and so on. This generality of the symbolic representation makes it very powerful, but it also makes it confusing. All the different meanings of *three quarters*, and the interconnections between them, need to be recognised and discussed – and, as always, represented in a way that can be grasped and recalled by learners who think more easily in pictures than in words.

b) *n n*ths Make a Whole One

If we want to do anything with the parts that fractions represent – if we want to add or subtract them, for example – then we must first make sure that they are all made up of the same-sized bits. We cannot add

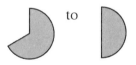, for instance, because these two fractions are different sizes and shapes. We must first break up the *two thirds* and the *half* into pieces that are all the same size. If we break the *two thirds* into four pieces, and the *half* into three, then all our pieces will be the same size and shape – they will all be *sixths*.

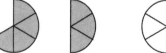

Now all the pieces will fit together properly, because they are all the same size and shape. There are seven of them altogether – four from the *two thirds* and three from the *half* – so the total is *seven sixths*, or *one whole and one sixth*.

The key concept here, one that needs to be rehearsed and emphasised in a lot of different contexts, is that *n n*ths *make a whole one*. This applies no matter what constitutes the 'whole one'. It might be a circular 'pizza' like the ones illustrated above, or a step one unit long on a number line, or a number of objects – a dozen eggs, say, or a bag of apples. Learners need plenty of experience of breaking up whole ones into *n n*ths, physically and mentally, so they learn not just *that* $1/4$ is less than $1/3$, and $1/96$ is less than $1/57$, but *why*. There are more quarters than thirds in the whole one, so each quarter must be smaller than a third.

PowerPoint

PowerPoint 5-1, *n n^{th}s Make a Whole One*, builds up the learners' understanding of the generalisation, from two halves, three thirds, four quarters, and so on, to 'sproog sprooths', and so to '*n n^{th}s*'. After working through the numbers, invite learners to invent absurd examples for themselves – beedle beedleths, corky corkieths, whatever whatever'ths! Have fun with the idea: it all helps to develop the key concept, that no matter what number *n* may be, *n n^{th}s make a whole one*.

In the Classroom – *n n^{th}s Make a Whole One*

Learners can make a poster showing examples of shapes divided into a number of equal parts. This will help to reinforce standard exercises on the use of conventional fraction notation.

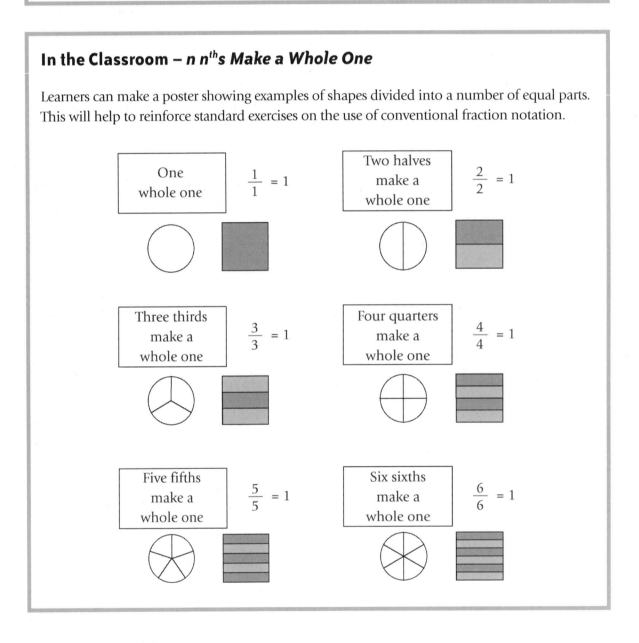

c) Equivalent Fractions

Once learners understand – really *understand* – the idea that *n n^{th}s make a whole one* they will be ready to work with equivalent fractions.

Now, textbooks often start by using diagrams to show how a lot of little bits may be put together to make a smaller number of bigger bits. So, for example, 6 shaded bits out of 8, or 6/8 of a whole one, may be put together to make 3 shaded bits out of 4. So 6/8 is equivalent to 3/4.

This is the diagrammatic equivalent of 'cancelling down' 6/8 to 3/4 – and as far as it goes, it is fine. But it is really the wrong way round. It starts from something that is harder to just 'see', the 6 shaded bits out of 8, and changes it to something that is easier, the 3 shaded bits out of 4.

But supposing we go the other way? We can start from the 3/4, and cut up the quarters into smaller equal-sized bits to make more of them. For example, we can cut each of the quarters in half.

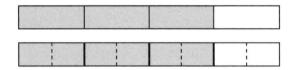

Now there are eight equal-sized bits in the whole one – so they must be eighths, because *n n^{th}s make a whole one*. So we have doubled the number of bits in the whole one, from 4 to 8. And what has happened to the number of shaded bits? That has doubled too! Why?

This approach is the reverse of 'cancelling down', but it may offer a clearer *model to think with* on which learners can base their understanding of equivalent fractions.

In the Classroom – *Equivalent Fractions*

Learners can start with a lot of equal-sized strips of paper, and fold them into quarters. They shade in three of the four quarters, and agree that three quarters of the strip are now shaded.

Then they choose a number of smaller bits to cut the four quarters up into. This can be done with scissors, or just by folding and drawing in the fold lines. They should always check the number of smaller bits that have now been made, and the number of these that are shaded.

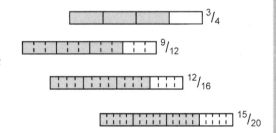

Ask learners to try cutting or folding the quarters up into different numbers of equal-sized bits. They can use formal notation to record their results, putting the number of shaded bits at the top of the fraction, and the number of bits in the whole at the bottom.

Encourage learners to see for themselves what is happening – that if you double the number of bits in the whole one, you double the number that are shaded. If you multiply the number of bits by three, or four, or five, then you multiply the number of shaded bits by the same number.

Each of the strips shows a fraction that is equivalent to 3/4. Learners may go on to start from other common fractions, such as 1/2 or 2/3, and find sets of equivalent fractions for these. The strips may be put together to make a poster.

d) Calculating with Fractions

With a thorough grasp of the mathematical concepts underlying equivalent fractions – not just a lot of 'rules' for 'cancelling down' – learners may go on to develop the four rules for fractions using diagrams to *justify* and *explain* each step of the operation.

Here again, most textbooks introduce the four rules for fractions using a diagrammatic approach. For example:

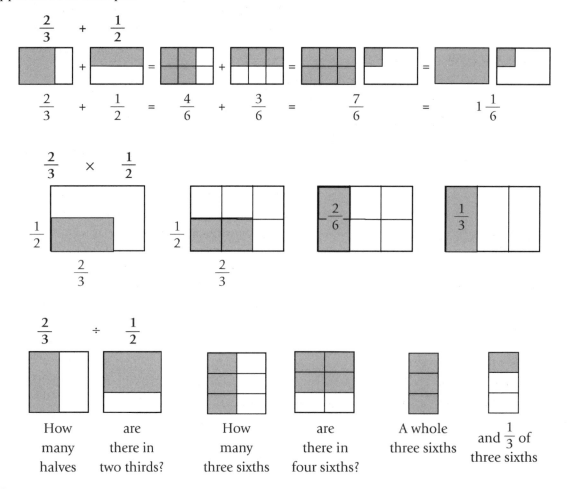

Diagrams like these are certainly helpful to visual and kinaesthetic thinkers. But they are often abandoned much too quickly, before the learner has had time to establish a 'picture in the mind' on which to hang their understanding, not just of the particular computation involved in the individual question, but of the whole principle of the addition or multiplication of fractions. Instead, they are given rules expressed in words and numbers – which they promptly forget.

But an understanding of the rules for manipulating the symbols can be based on an understanding of the graphics. If the connections between the graphics and the rules are made clear then learners who cannot recall the rules but can recall the graphics for a simple example can work out the rest for themselves when they need to.

In each of the tables below, the column on the left shows how the shapes are manipulated for one operation – addition, multiplication or division. The column on the right describes the same manipulation, but in terms of numbers and symbols. The aim should be to develop the learners' understanding of the connections between the two.

So, for example, the picture for the addition or subtraction of fractions is of breaking up two different sized and shaped fractions of a whole in order to fit them together neatly. Finding a common denominator is the numerical and symbolic equivalent of this process.

Adding Fractions

Using Graphics	*Using Rules*
*To **add two fractions** of a whole,* *e.g.*	*To **add two fractions**,* *e.g.* $\dfrac{2}{3} + \dfrac{1}{2}$
you break them up into same-sized bits *e.g.*	*you give them a common denominator by multiplying the numerator and the denominator by the same multiplier* *e.g.* $\dfrac{4}{6} + \dfrac{3}{6}$
and then you put the bits together *e.g.*	*and then you add the two numerators* *e.g.* $\dfrac{7}{6}$
into whole ones and the biggest same-sized bits you can. *e.g.*	*and then you cancel down and make a mixed number.* *e.g.* $1\dfrac{1}{6}$

For multiplication we use the area model again, just as for the multiplication of whole numbers (see Chapter 3, *Models for Multiplication and Division*).

Multiplying Fractions

Using Graphics	*Using Rules*
To multiply two fractions of a whole, you draw the two fractions of a line, *e.g.*	*To multiply two fractions,* *e.g.* $\quad \dfrac{2}{3} \quad \times \quad \dfrac{1}{2}$
then you draw the rectangle with the two fractions of a line as its edges *e.g.*	*you multiply the two numerators together and the two denominators together* *e.g.* $\quad \dfrac{2 \times 1}{3 \times 2}$
and find its area *e.g.*	*e.g.* $\quad \dfrac{2}{6}$
using the biggest same-sized bits you can. *e.g.*	*and then you cancel down.* *e.g.* $\quad \dfrac{1}{3}$

The diagrams for both addition and multiplication lead directly to the standard rules for the addition and multiplication of fractions. The picture for the division of fractions, on the other hand, does not lead to the 'turning upside down' method that learners are often asked to commit to memory with little or no understanding. It offers a different – and more meaningful – approach. We start by taking 'division' in its 'How many are there in ...?' sense, rather than its 'sharing' sense (see Chapter 3, *Models for Multiplication and Division*). So $2/3 \div 1/2$, for example, means *How many halves are there in two thirds?*

Dividing Fractions

Using Graphics	*Using Rules*
To divide one fraction of a whole by another e.g. How many halves are there in two thirds?	*To divide one fraction by another* e.g. $\dfrac{2}{3} \div \dfrac{1}{2}$
you break them up into same-sized bits so you can compare them easily e.g. How many three sixths are there in four sixths?	*you give them a common denominator by multiplying the numerator and the denominator by the same multiplier* e.g. $\dfrac{4}{6} \div \dfrac{3}{6}$
and then you see how many of the first set of bits there are in the second. e.g. A whole and $\frac{1}{3}$ of three sixths three sixths	*and then you divide the first numerator by the second numerator* e.g. $4 \div 3$, or $\dfrac{4}{3}$
	and then you cancel down and make a mixed number. e.g. $1\frac{1}{3}$

Using this approach, the two fractions are first *given a common denominator* (or, in graphical terms, *broken up into the same-sized bits*), just as they are for an addition.

$$\frac{2}{3} \div \frac{1}{2}$$
$$= \frac{4}{6} \div \frac{3}{6}$$

Now we have a simple division – *How many of the second fraction are there in the first?* Because the two fractions are made up of the same-sized bits they are directly comparable so we are just asking, *How many of the second set of bits do we need to make the first?*, or *What is the first set divided by the second?* This translates back into the symbolic and numerical rule, *Divide the first numerator by the second.*

$$\frac{4}{6} \div \frac{3}{6}$$
$$= 4 \div 3$$

In each case, for addition (or subtraction), multiplication and division, the 'picture in the mind' makes sense of the method. This makes it possible for the visual and kinaesthetic thinker to work out *how* to carry out the calculation by recalling *why* the method works.

Theme: Making Links – Explanation, Justification and Proof

The processes of explanation and justification form the basis of mathematical *proof*. They are relevant at every level and in every area of mathematics, but they are particularly valuable for those topics, of which Fractions is a prime example, that are peculiarly prone to teaching and learning by rule-based rote. Learners may know *how* to solve a routine problem, but be quite unable to explain *why* the method they are using works. A model or a diagram will very often open the door to the *why*, even for learners who are, at least for a time, capable of recalling and reproducing the steps for the *how*. Using diagrams or models to explain *why* involves significantly higher order thinking skills than calculating with figures, and the process lays a firm foundation for further work in mathematical proof as opposed to routine calculation.

---

e) The Clock Face – Another Useful Model

Another useful model for work with fractions, and one that is connected with other areas of the mathematics curriculum, is the analogue clock face. This is divided into twelve equal sections, conveniently labelled 1 to 12. The minute hand of the clock turns through a quarter turn to the three, and a half turn to the six, to show 'quarter past' and 'half past' the hour. So there we are, even before we have begun to learn about fractions, with *three twelfths* and *six twelfths* equal to a *quarter* and a *half* – all from learning to tell the time.

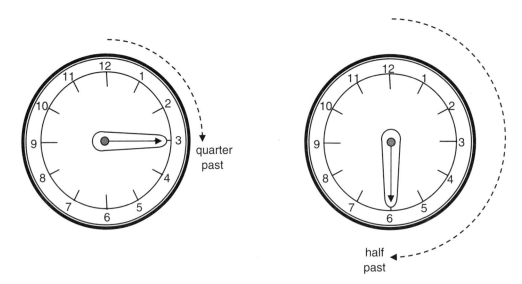

quarter past

half past

The other fractions on a clock face are not commonly used in the context of time – we do not usually say *three quarters past four*, or *one third past seven*. But these, along with sixths and twelfths, may be demonstrated using a clock face cut out of card with a 'hand' attached with a split-pin paper fastener. The standard analogue clock face is useful only for computations involving halves, thirds, quarters, sixths and twelfths – but these are enough to establish a feel for what it means to add and subtract fractions.

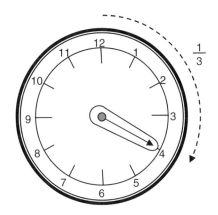

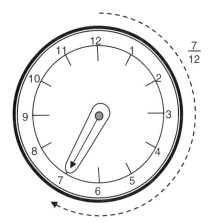

Learners may have their own smaller versions of the clock face with a rotating hand, cut out of card. Resource Sheets 5-1, *Large Fraction Clock*, and 5-2, *Small Fraction Clocks*, can be used to prepare these materials.

In the Classroom – *Clock-Face Fractions*

The clock face may be used to add and subtract halves, thirds, quarters, sixths and twelfths.

To start with, learners will need to use the physical model of the clock face for computations like these. But later, when the visual and kinaesthetic 'picture in the mind' has become firmly established, they can learn to work visually, using a mental image to imagine the clock hand moving around the clock face.

This is a quick and flexible method for the solution of such problems as $^1/4 + {}^1/3$ or $^2/3 - {}^5/12$, which, like any meaningful piece of mathematics, is much easier to recall than a rote-learnt rule.

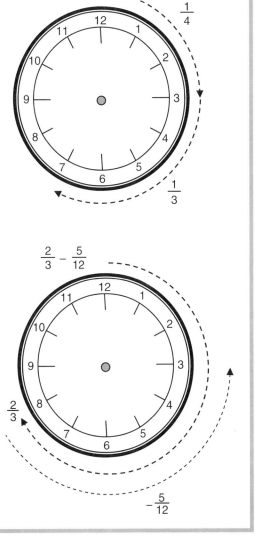

Fractions – Teaching Points

- Shapes and patterns may be used to represent fractions, and these will help to give the symbols meaning.

- The symbolic representation of a fraction can carry a range of different meanings, and these need to be identified and understood.

- The key concept is that *n nths make a whole one*.

- The 'four rules' for fractions are commonly presented as a set of instructions for manipulating numbers and symbols.

- Diagrams for operations on fractions give the *why* as well as the *how*.

- A useful image for the addition, subtraction and division of fractions is of chopping the fractions up into equal-sized bits which can then be combined or compared directly.

- The multiplication of fractions can be understood with an area model.

- A clock face offers another useful model for the addition and subtraction of fractions.

- When the symbols have meaning learners can understand, not just learn, the 'four rules' for fractions.

Resources on the CD

Mathematical PowerPoints

　　PP 5-1 *n nths Make a Whole One*

　　PP 5-2 *Fractions and Repeating Patterns*

Resource Sheets

　　RS 5-1 *Large Fraction Clock*

　　RS 5-2 *Small Fraction Clocks*

Further Reading and Resources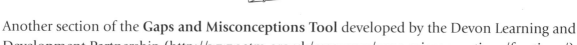

Another section of the **Gaps and Misconceptions Tool** developed by the Devon Learning and Development Partnership (http://www.atm.org.uk/resources/gaps-misconceptions/fractions/) offers readings and resources to support teachers in their work on Fractions and Decimals.

CHAPTER 6

Ratio, Proportion and Percentages

> **Some key concepts**
>
> ■ Ratio and proportion are all about things keeping the same shape when they get bigger or smaller.
>
> ■ A *proportion* is out of the whole, while a *ratio* is of one part to another.
>
> ■ If you make a rectangle bigger you must keep the lengths of its sides in proportion. Otherwise it will be distorted – it will become a different shape.
>
> ■ A percentage is a 'proportion out of a hundred'.

a) Picturing Ratios

The concept of ratio is complex. It is normally introduced in the context of relationships between sets of numbers, rather than lengths or shapes – but this may make it more confusing for learners who think more readily in pictures than in words and symbols. Learners are expected to understand the idea of a *ratio* between two numbers, such as *two to three*, long before they meet the concept of a pair of *similar shapes*, one of which is an enlargement of the other. For visual and kinaesthetic thinkers this may be the wrong way round.

For example, take a purely numerical problem:

Two bottles of soda weigh three kilos. What do four bottles of soda weigh?

This may be represented as:

2:3 = 4:?

There are four numbers to think about here – 2, 3 and 4 are given, and ? must be found. The learner must realise that the relationship between the 2 and the 3 is the same as the relationship between the 4 and the ?, and that the relationship between the 2 and the 4 is the same as the relationship between the 3 and the ?, but the relationship between the 3 and the 4, or the 2 and the ?, is irrelevant. Working out which relationship is which, and which ones matter, is difficult. They are, after all, just a lot of numbers. It is not obvious which 'go together', or why.

But if instead the problem relates to a pair of mathematically similar shapes then the numbers may make better sense. For example, the numerical problem *2:3 = 4:?* may be presented in the context of a pair of rectangles. The first rectangle has a height of

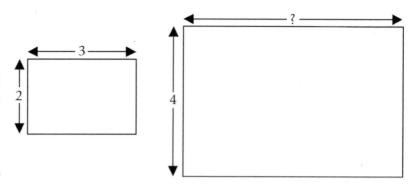

2 units and a width of 3 units. The second rectangle is exactly the same shape as the first. It is just bigger. It is twice as high as the smaller rectangle, but it has not changed its shape. It has just grown steadily. So if it is twice as high then it must also be twice as wide.

Now the important relationships – the pairs of numbers that 'go together' – can be identified from the rectangles. The width of the first rectangle is one and a half times its height – so the second rectangle must also have a width that is one and a half times its height. That is, the relationship between the *2* and the *3* (the ratio *2:3*) must be the same as the relationship between the *4* and the *?* (the ratio *4:?*). Again, the height of the second rectangle is twice the height of the first, so the width of the second rectangle must also be twice the width of the first. That is, the relationship between the *2* and the *4* (the ratio *2:4*) must be the same as the relationship between the *3* and the *?* (the ratio *3:?*). Either way I can get a feel for the size of the *?*, before I calculate it more exactly as *6*. If we change the height of any rectangle then we must also change its width, or it will distort and become a different shape. But there is clearly no reason to focus on the relationship between the *3* and the *4*, or between the *2* and the *?*, because this would involve comparing the width of one rectangle with the height of the other.

In the Classroom – *Similar Shapes*

The model of a shape that 'grows' but does not distort may be reinforced with plenty of graphical examples.

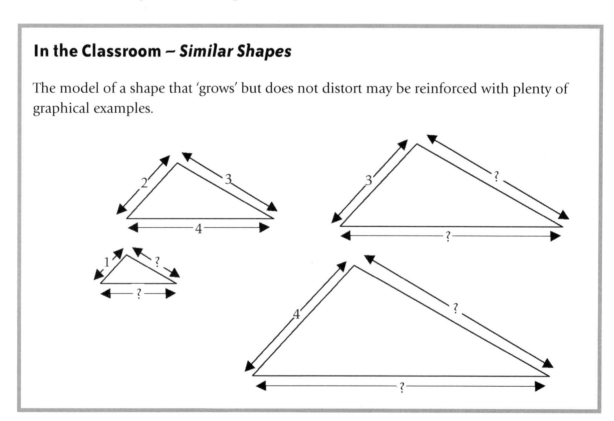

If learners have access to a drawing package on a computer, then holding down the shift key and dragging one corner of any shape will cause it to shrink or expand without distorting. This moving image provides a vivid 'picture in the mind' on which learners may base their understanding of ratio.

b) Proportion

Another useful image to help learners to picture ratio and proportion is the idea of 'bundles'. The problem *2:3 = 4:?* may be represented with 'bundles' of two – with two bundles of, say, white cubes, and three bundles of grey. This gives two white to three grey *bundles*, but it also gives four white to six grey *cubes*. If each of the bundles contained more cubes then there could be six white to nine grey cubes, or twenty white to thirty grey cubes, or whatever, but there would still be only two white to three grey bundles, so all these ratios are equivalent.

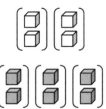

Theme: Making Links – Equivalent Ratios and Equivalent Fractions

The image of bundles is similar to the repeating patterns that were referred to in PowerPoint 5-2 *Fractions and Repeating Patterns* in Chapter 5, *Fractions*. The repeating patterns provide an image of equivalent fractions, while the bundles give rise to equivalent ratios.

The image of bundles is particularly useful in helping learners to understand the concept of proportion, and its connection with *fraction of*. The terms *ratio* and *proportion* go together, but they mean different things. A *proportion* is out of the whole, while a *ratio* is of one part to another. The picture of the bundles of cubes allows us to use the different terms in a way that brings out their connected meanings.

There are 2 white cubes for every 3 grey cubes.
There are 3 grey cubes for every 2 white cubes.

The ratio of white cubes to grey cubes is 2 to 3, or 2:3.
The ratio of grey cubes to white cubes is 3 to 2, or 3:2.

The proportion of white cubes is 2 out of 5. 2/5 of the cubes are white.
The proportion of grey cubes is 3 out of 5. 3/5 of the cubes are grey.

The image of the bundles of cubes may seem easier to understand than the similar rectangles. An example like this, perhaps involving bundles of apples and pears, or the ingredients for a recipe, rather than different colours of cubes, is common in primary mathematics textbooks. But the bundles model is heavily dependent on numbers, and it may, for that reason, be less appropriate as an introduction to ratio and proportion for learners who find numbers difficult to comprehend. The image of a shape, growing or shrinking but never distorting, is easier to manipulate mentally. I can make a shape grow, or shrink, in one easy movement. The kinaesthetic experience is smooth and comfortable. On the other hand, the bundles showing the connection between the ratios

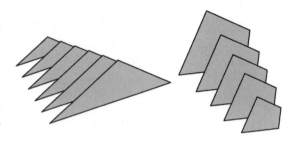

twelve to sixteen, eighteen to twenty-four, and three to four, for example, are more fiddly. I am likely to loose track of the difference between the numbers of bundles (the *3:4*) and the numbers of white and grey cubes (the *12:16* and the *18:24*) in the picture. Shapes that grow and shrink offer a more holistic model. This may help visual and kinaesthetic learners to grasp the principle of ratio, without having to worry about specific numbers of cubes and bundles.

12:16 = 3:4

18:24 = 3:4

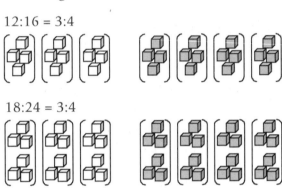

In the Classroom – *Maps and Scale*

Maps and scale models provide a useful context for the development of learners' understanding of proportion.

A series of maps or aerial photographs, each covering the position of the school at a different scale, will convey a sense of 'zooming in' which can help learners to develop an understanding of scale. These could range from a plan of the solar system or a satellite picture on a very small scale, through a selection of maps or photographs to a large scale plan or photograph of the classroom. Maps centring on the school may be downloaded and printed off from the web. Google Earth provides an excellent tool to develop learners' understanding of scale. (See *Further Reading and Resources* below.)

Some learners may find it interesting to consider how some dolls are distorted, while others are fairly accurate scale models. It is commonly reported that if a Barbie doll were a full size woman, she would be about six foot tall and, at 50 kilos, seriously underweight (see *Further Reading and Resources* below). What conclusions may be drawn about other dolls?

A collection of cereal boxes, from the 'individual portion' to the 'giant' 750 gram or 1 kilo size, can present an interesting problem. Are all the boxes the same shape (that is, mathematically similar), or do they distort as they change size? The same question may be asked about a set of Russian dolls, or larger and smaller mineral water or soft drink bottles.

c) Percentages

A percentage is a proportion. It is what a fraction would be, if it were out of a hundred. So to convert a fraction to a percentage we must divide the whole up into a hundred parts. This can be represented with a hundred-unit percentage grid superimposed on the whole.

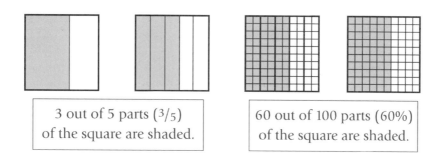

3 out of 5 parts (³/₅) of the square are shaded.

60 out of 100 parts (60%) of the square are shaded.

Or we can use the Slavonic abacus again.

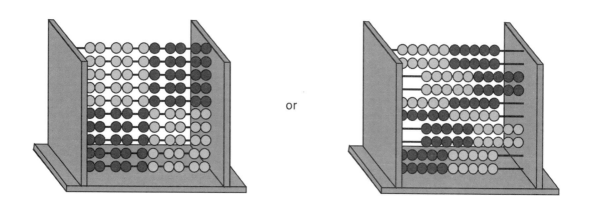

or

But the problem with converting many fractions into percentages is that they do not map easily onto a proportion of a hundred. When the fraction is a proportion of a factor or a multiple of a hundred it is not too difficult. The hundred-unit percentage grid can be manipulated to fit neatly over the parts of the original fraction. So 9 out of 25, for example, can be seen as 36 out of a hundred, or 36%.

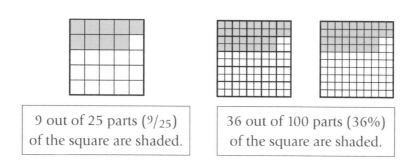

9 out of 25 parts (⁹/₂₅) of the square are shaded.

36 out of 100 parts (36%) of the square are shaded.

Similarly, a proportion of 200 can be represented by stretching the percentage grid out to show that each 'one percent' covers 2 out of the 200.

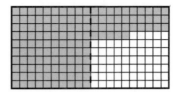

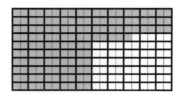

| 135 out of 200 parts ($^{135}/_{200}$) of the rectangle are shaded. | 67.5 out of 100 parts (67.5%) of the rectangle are shaded. |

But a hundred does not have many factors. Compared to 144, say, or 360, it has very few. Many real problems involve proportions that cannot be represented by whole number percentages – that is, by a whole number 'out of a hundred'. Hampered as we are with ten fingers and thumbs, our number system is inevitably clumsy because the base we use is not easily divisible by anything but multiples of 2 or 5. When the denominator of the fraction to be converted is not a factor or a multiple of a hundred it can be difficult to 'see' how the hundred-unit percentage grid can be made to fit over it.

The picture for 7 out of 15, for example, is more complicated. The hundred units of the percentage grid will not fit neatly over the fifteenths in the fraction. Forty-six of the unit squares are covered completely, but an odd third of each of two unit squares in the percentage grid have to be added together to give $^2/_3$, or 0.6666.....

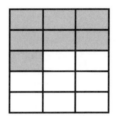

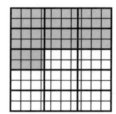

| 7 out of 15 parts ($^7/_{15}$) of the rectangle are shaded. | 46 $^2/_3$ out of 100 parts (46.6̇%) of the rectangle are shaded. |

And even a common, straightforward fraction like $^1/_3$ gives an awkward, 'bitty' picture which leads to a fraction or a repeating decimal in the equivalent percentage.

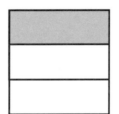

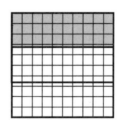

| 1 out of 3 parts ($^1/_3$) of the rectangle are shaded. | 33 $^1/_3$ out of 100 parts (33.3̇%) of the rectangle are shaded. |

Here there are ten odd thirds that have to be combined to make $3^1/_3$, which must then be added to the 30 unit squares that are completely shaded in the hundred-unit percentage grid.

So the concept of a percentage may be difficult for visual and kinaesthetic thinkers to grasp. They may understand that, when using a percentage, they are expressing a proportion out of a hundred rather than out of some other convenient whole number. *Per cent*, after all, means *per hundred – out of a hundred*. Using a common denominator – that is, splitting each of the 'wholes' into the same number of parts – makes it easy to compare the relative sizes of the different fractions. But a hundred is a clumsy number to use to divide up the wholes. Its use is a matter of convention, leading directly from our decimal number system, but it is likely to cause learners who think more easily in pictures and models than in words and symbols some difficulty. It is not easy to create the visual and kinaesthetic 'pictures in the mind' needed to think effectively about percentages.

Theme: Making Links – Fractions, Decimals and Percentages

Most mathematics textbooks have a table showing the equivalences between some common fractions, decimals and percentages. There may be a poster displayed in the classroom showing some of these number facts. But what these tables and posters lack is any explanation of the *why* that underlies the *how*. Here again, we need a picture that will link together the three concepts – fractions,

$\dfrac{1}{4}$	$\dfrac{3}{10}$	$\dfrac{1}{3}$
0.25	0.3	$0.\dot{3}$
25%	30%	$33.\dot{3}\%$

decimals, and percentages. It is not immediately obvious, for example, what ¹/₄ has to do with 25%. The two symbolic representations do not have a single squiggle in common. But a simple diagram can make the connection clear.

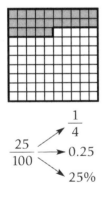

$$\dfrac{25}{100} \nearrow \dfrac{1}{4}$$
$$\dfrac{25}{100} \rightarrow 0.25$$
$$\dfrac{25}{100} \searrow 25\%$$

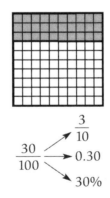

$$\dfrac{30}{100} \nearrow \dfrac{3}{10}$$
$$\dfrac{30}{100} \rightarrow 0.30$$
$$\dfrac{30}{100} \searrow 30\%$$

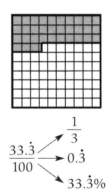

$$\dfrac{33.\dot{3}}{100} \nearrow \dfrac{1}{3}$$
$$\dfrac{33.\dot{3}}{100} \rightarrow 0.\dot{3}$$
$$\dfrac{33.\dot{3}}{100} \searrow 33.\dot{3}\%$$

The key here is in the use of the hundred-unit square. The poster stating the equivalences may seem to summarise what the diagrams show – but to visual and kinaesthetic learners it is the diagrams, rather than the lists of symbols, that summarise each set of relationships.

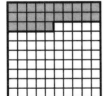 is meaningful and memorable, but ¹/₄ = 0.25 = 25% is not.

(Continued)

(Continued)

As always, the focus, at least for the spatial thinkers in the classroom, must be on developing their understanding of the relationships. Then even if they cannot recall the equivalences, they will have a way to work these out for themselves.

In the Classroom – *Fractions, Decimals and Percentages*

Learners can make a series of posters, each one based on a partially shaded hundred square, with the shading expressed as a fraction out of a hundred, a fraction in its lowest terms, a decimal and a percentage. Where the percentage is a whole number it may also be shown on the Slavonic abacus.

Ratio, Proportion and Percentages – Teaching Points

- Ratio and proportion are usually presented as primarily numerical concepts. This may make them hard for visual and kinaesthetic thinkers to grasp.

- For visual and kinaesthetic thinkers, the concept of mathematical similarity holds the key to understanding ratio.

- Similar shapes offer a useful 'picture in the mind' for ratio.

- Images of 'bundles' are useful to bring out the relationship between ratio and proportion.

- It can be difficult to see how the whole will split into a hundred parts, so percentages may be difficult for spatial thinkers to visualise and understand.

- The hundred-unit percentage grid brings together fractions, decimals and percentages, and helps to show how these are interrelated.

Further Reading and Resources

A range of resources may be used to develop learners' understanding of Scale. **Maps** with different scales may be printed off from www.streetmap.co.uk. Google Earth, at http://www.google.co.uk/intl/en_uk/earth/index.html, allows the viewer to zoom in to the local area, and then to pull further and further away to see how this is positioned in the surrounding area, in the country, in the whole continent and finally on earth.

A discussion of the Barbie doll statistics may be found at http://en.wikipedia.org/wiki/Barbie#Controversies.

CHAPTER 7

Algebra

Some key concepts

- An algebraic symbol, such as x, can be used in different ways. It can represent a specific, unknown value, or it can represent a variable which can be given a range of alternative values.

- The equals sign means 'the total value of everything on one side of the '=' is equal to the total value of everything on the other side'. It does **not** mean 'Work this out and find the answer'!

- An equation must be kept balanced. Whatever we do on one side, we must do the same thing on the other.

- An algebraic expression represents something – for example, the area of a shape or the number of counters in the nth member of a sequence.

---

a) Using Symbols

Algebra is full of symbols. The quintessential algebraic symbol for most people – adults as well as children – is x. x crops up all over the place, with different meanings and different values in different situations. This can be very confusing.

x can represent one or more specific values in an equation. These values are (at least to begin with) unknown, but it may be possible to work out what they are – so in $4 + x = 10$, for example, x is 6, but in $x^2 = 9$ it is 3 or -3. x has different values in different equations, but only one value, or a particular set of values, in any one equation.

But x can also represent the variable in a function. You can choose different input values for x, and these will produce different outputs. So in the function $y = x + 3$, for example, y is 4 when x is 1, but y is 96 when x is 93.

These two uses of an algebraic symbol such as x, in an equation where it has a specific, unknown value, and in a function where it serves as a variable that can take different values, need to be understood. So for early work in algebra the first thing we need is a symbol that indicates clearly, in itself, the range of meanings and values that x can have. Some textbooks use a box for the unknown when equations are introduced, with $4 + \square = 10$, for example, or $\square - 7 = 2$. This is helpful, as the boxes are closed so we do not know what is inside, but we may be able to open them to find out. The variable in a function, on the other hand, may be thought of as a box into which we can put a range of values – so in $\blacksquare = \square + 3$ we have a function relating the variable $\blacksquare$ to the variable $\square$, where the number in $\blacksquare$ is always three more than the number in $\square$. Then, with time, the more conventional letters can be introduced, with $y = x + 3$, for example.

b) Solving Equations – the Balancing Model

The equality sign has a very clear meaning. It means that the total value of everything on one side of the '=' is equal to the total value of everything on the other side.

That, at least, is the theory. But what many learners understand by the equality sign is the instruction: *Work out the answer*. They meet thousands of such orders over a period of years in exercises set out with an equality sign and an answer space: $3 + 6 =$ _____ ; $4 \times 9 + 17 =$ _____ ; $16\pi - \sqrt{(3.6)} =$ _____ ; $(x + 3)(x + 1) =$ _____ ; and so on. In each case, the equality sign actually carries the message *Do the calculation on the left, and write the answer on the right*. This can lead to such nonsensical working as:

$$4 \times 9 + 17 = 4 \times 9 = 36 + 17 = 53$$

The real meaning of the equality sign should be discussed early, before the introduction of formal algebra. The visual and kinaesthetic 'picture in the mind' that we need here is a well-established one, and it is very effective. It shows a set of balancing scales, which must be kept balanced by ensuring that the total value of everything in each of the two pans is equal.

This image is very powerful. If it is firmly established early on it will help to discourage learners from representing a series of non-equivalent expressions as though they were all equal, as in the nonsensical working above. Since there is a pan on each side the equivalences work both ways, giving both $3 + 6 = 9$, and $9 = 3 + 6$. The former represents the aggregation of two groups, and the latter a partitioning of a whole number. The concept of the balance helps to discourage the use of meaningless rules for algebraic manipulation, such as *change sides, change sign*. As always, it is the meaning that underlies the symbols that must be the focus of attention, not a set of rules for their manipulation.

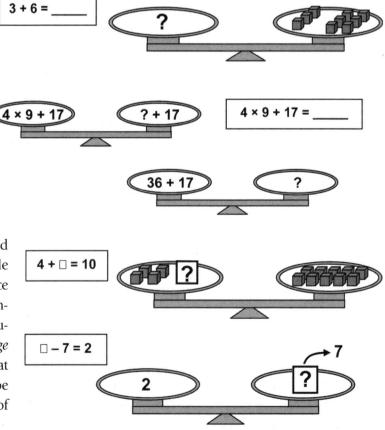

PowerPoint

PowerPoint 7-1, *Balancing,* shows how a simple equation may be 'solved' with a series of steps, but always keeping the value of the two pans equal to ensure that the scales remain balanced.

c) Simple Algebraic Expressions

Just as numbers may be understood holistically, as patterns of dots on a Slavonic abacus, so algebraic expressions may be given a graphical meaning that will help learners who think more easily in pictures than in words and symbols to understand and work with them effectively.

In the Classroom – *Writing Simple Algebraic Expressions*

Learners can use shapes with areas expressed algebraically to make simple patterns, then express the total areas of their patterns algebraically.

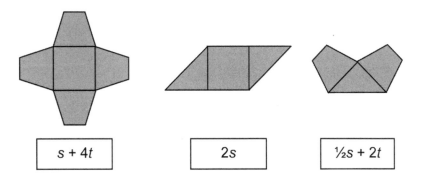

They may be challenged to make two or more patterns with areas that are represented by the same algebraic expression.

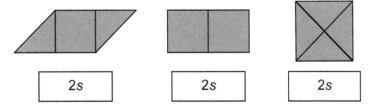

This gives a kinaesthetic and visual meaning to the process of 'collecting like terms' in a valid mathematical context.

PowerPoint

PowerPoint 7-2, *Tangram Algebra*, presents an activity using the perimeters of Tangram Tiles as a meaningful context for the construction of simple algebraic expressions.

Resource Sheet 7-1, *Tangram Tiles*, provides outlines for sets of the tiles.

---

d) Generalised Algebraic Expressions

A sequence of patterns that grow according to a regular rule offers a useful context for writing a meaningful generalised expression. The algebraic expression for the nth member of the sequence can be pulled directly out of the patterns. The sequence can start simply, but combine and build up to more elaborate patterns which are represented by complex, but still meaningful, expressions.

In the Classroom – *Generalised Expressions from Sequences*

Learners can make a sequence of simple patterns of counters, then use this as a basis for more complex patterns. For example, Pattern n in this sequence is made of n^2 counters.

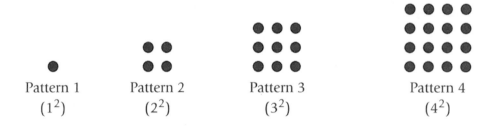

| Pattern 1 | Pattern 2 | Pattern 3 | Pattern 4 |
| (1^2) | (2^2) | (3^2) | (4^2) |

Adding 4 counters to each pattern gives a related sequence. Pattern n in this sequence is made of $n^2 + 4$ counters.

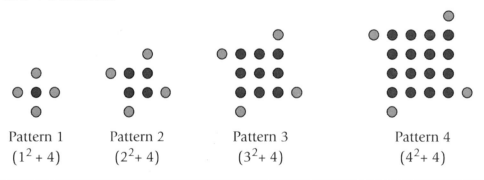

| Pattern 1 | Pattern 2 | Pattern 3 | Pattern 4 |
| $(1^2 + 4)$ | $(2^2 + 4)$ | $(3^2 + 4)$ | $(4^2 + 4)$ |

Or we can double up on the original sequence, to get a sequence of patterns made with $2n^2$ counters.

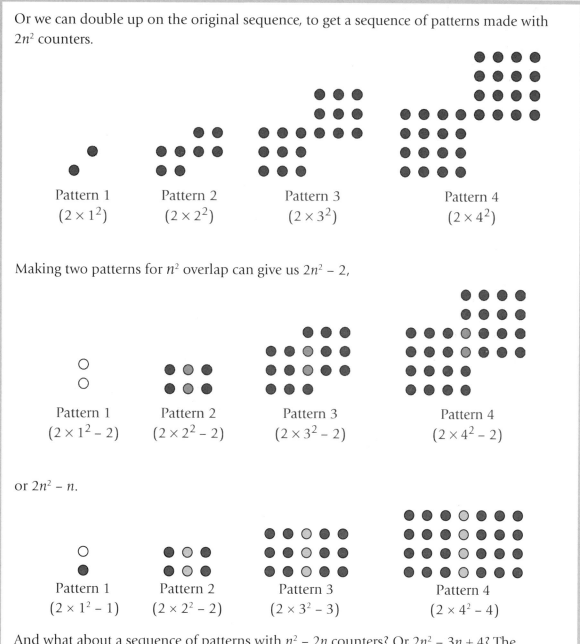

Making two patterns for n^2 overlap can give us $2n^2 - 2$,

or $2n^2 - n$.

And what about a sequence of patterns with $n^2 - 2n$ counters? Or $2n^2 - 3n + 4$? The possibilities are endless – but each expression, no matter how complex, has meaning when it is used to express the number of counters in the nth member of a sequence of patterns.

If algebraic expressions mean something then the rules for algebraic manipulation will make much more sense. A sequence of patterns can be shaded in different ways to show why two expressions which look very different may be equivalent. For example, the counters in the sequence of patterns:

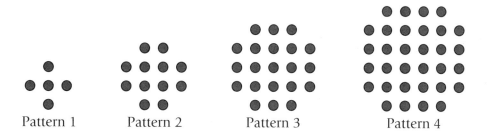

may be coloured to show that Pattern n in the sequence has $n^2 + 4n$ counters:

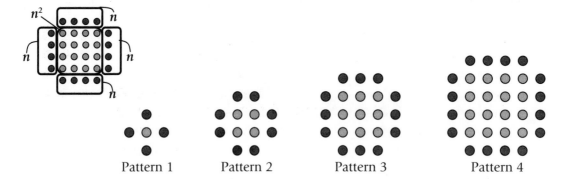

Alternatively, they may be coloured to show that it has $n(n + 2) + 2n$ counters:

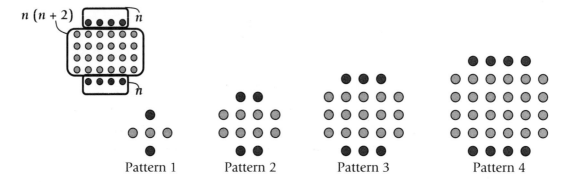

Or, with attention drawn to the 'missing' counters in the corners, the number of counters in Pattern n can be seen to be $(n + 2)^2 - 4$:

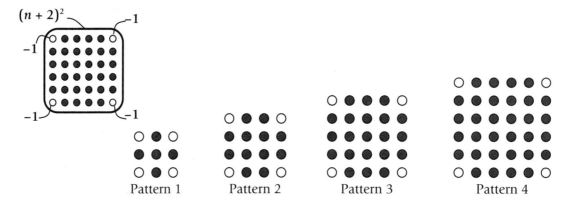

These diagrams are a graphical representation of the algebraic equivalences,

$$n^2 + 4n = n(n + 2) + 2n = (n + 2)^2 - 4.$$

In each case, the expression can be pulled directly out of the structure of the sequence of patterns. Each part of the expression can be related back to the relevant sections of the pattern, to give it a meaning that can be seen and understood.

e) Multiplying Algebraic Expressions

We have seen how the physical and spatial concept of the *area of a rectangle* can help learners to put meaning into both single-digit and long multiplication (see Chapter 3, *Models for Multiplication and Division*). The same approach may be used to explain what we are doing when we multiply two fractions (see Chapter 5, *Fractions*). Now this invaluable 'picture in the mind' makes another appearance, as we come to multiply a pair of algebraic expressions.

Algebraic expressions may be multiplied out sequentially, taking pairs of terms, one from each expression, in turn. For example:

$$(x + 3)(x + 1) = x^2 + x + 3x + 3 = x^2 + 4x + 3$$

Provided learners keep track of the pairs of terms this will generally lead to the right answer. But it may leave learners unsure why the method works. It may be clear where the x^2 comes from – after all, the x in one bracket has been multiplied by the x in the other. But why does the final expression contain all those loose x's? What do they mean? How are they different from the x^2?

Finding the area of a rectangle with sides of length $(x + 3)$ and $(x + 1)$ gives meaning to the whole process.

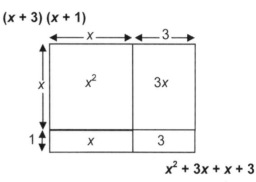

$$x^2 + 3x + x + 3$$

The expressions to be multiplied out may be more complex – for example:

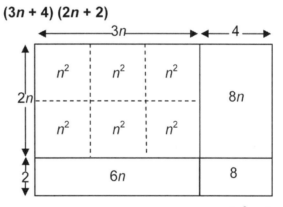

$$6n^2 + 8n + 6n + 8$$

If there are negative signs in the expressions then it is helpful to think in stages. For example, to find the area of a rectangle with sides of length $(a + 6)$ and $(a - 2)$, we first find the area of a rectangle with sides of length $(a + 6)$ and (a).

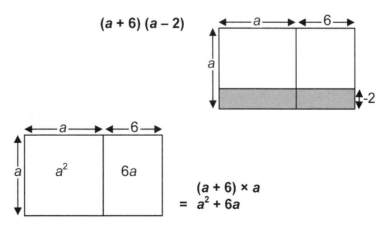

$$(a + 6) \times a$$
$$= a^2 + 6a$$

Then we strip off the two shaded rectangles that we do not want – one with sides a and 2, and the other with sides 6 and 2 …

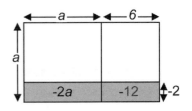

….to give $\quad a^2 + 6a - 2a - 12$

$\qquad\qquad = a^2 + 4a - 12$

Similarly, to find the area of a rectangle with sides of length $(m - 3)$ and $(m - 4)$,

$(m - 3)(m - 4)$

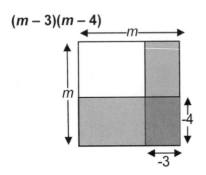

we start with a square with sides of length m.

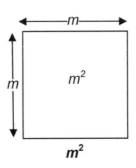

Then we strip off two rectangles – first one with sides of length m and 3

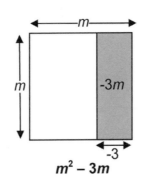

followed by a rectangle with sides of length m and 4.

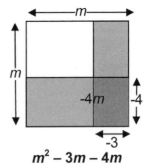

But now we have stripped off the darkly shaded rectangle in the bottom right-hand corner twice. This has sides of length 3 and 4, so this area, 12, must be added back on.

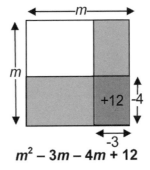

This gives us the expansion:

$(m - 3)(m - 4) = m^2$ (the m by m square, with nothing stripped off)

$\qquad$ **$- 3m$** (the 3 by m rectangle stripped off)

$\qquad$ **$- 4m$** (the 4 by m rectangle stripped off)

$\qquad$ **$+ 12$** (the doubly-stripped 3 by 4 rectangle replaced.)

The series of diagrams, like those for the previous calculations, not only enable us to expand a pair of brackets, but also to see where each term in the expansion comes from. Why are the terms in m negative? Because we stripped these rectangles away from the m by m square that we started with. Why is the final numerical term positive? Because we have to put back what we have stripped off twice. The whole thing makes sense.

PowerPoint

PowerPoint 7-3, *Multiplying out Brackets*, shows how a square with sides $(a + b)$ has an area of $a^2 + b^2 + 2ab$.

But here again, as so often in mathematics, understanding what is going on takes longer and is more demanding than simply learning a 'method' to get the 'right answer'. The so-called 'boxes method' – see below – may help some learners to keep track of the steps in the calculation, but it will do little to enable them to understand what they are doing. This example serves to demonstrate how easily an approach designed to foster learners' understanding of key mathematical concepts can be corrupted into yet another set of 'rules' for getting 'right answers' – meaningless, irrelevant, and altogether forgettable!

NOT to be used – *The 'Boxes' Method*

The area approach to the multiplication of two algebraic expressions can be corrupted quite easily into just another routine – the so-called 'boxes' method. This is nothing more than a way of laying out the computation. It does not show why both the terms in m are negative, nor why the '12' is positive. If anything, it is likely to prove more confusing than the linear layout, as it seems to suggest that all of the 'boxes' are the same size, and that three of them have one or more negative edge lengths. This method is more cumbersome, and takes longer to draw, than the conventional 'pairing off' routine. It has little to recommend it – and it will certainly not offer a 'picture in the mind' that will support learners' understanding of the principles that underlie the process of multiplying a pair of algebraic expressions.

$(m - 3)(m - 4)$

	m	-3
m	m^2	$-3m$
-4	$-4m$	12

Algebra – Teaching Points

- An algebraic x can have two different uses, as the unknown in an equation, or as a variable in a function. These different uses need to be understood.

- The equality sign, =, means that the total value of everything on one side of the symbol is equal to the total value of everything on the other. It does **not** mean 'Do this sum'.

- The balancing model is a valuable 'picture in the mind' to help learners to understand the meaning of the equality sign.

- Simple patterns and growing sequences can give meaning to simple and generalised algebraic expressions.

- The area model is once again useful in helping learners to understand what happens when a pair of algebraic expressions are multiplied together.

Resources on the CD

Mathematical PowerPoints

    PP 7-1 *Balancing*

    PP 7-2 *Tangram Algebra*

    PP 7-3 *Multiplying out Brackets*

Resource Sheet

    RS 7-1 *Tangram Tiles*

Further Reading and Resources

John Mason with Alan Graham and Sue Johnston Wilder, 2005: *Developing Thinking in Algebra*. Open University in association with Paul Chapman Publishing.
This book offers a range of tasks to develop learners' understanding of algebra, using both visual and symbolic representations.

Geoff Giles' excellent resource pack, *Algebra through Geometry*, is no longer available, but the key ideas form the basis of a set of activities that can be accessed through the NCETM website at https://www.ncetm.org.uk/resources/24352. You will need Resource Sheets 3, 4, 5 and 6 from this address.

A different activity, *Perimeter Expressions*, uses the perimeters of rectangles in the A paper-size series as a context for the development of meaningful algebraic expressions. This activity may be accessed on the NRICH website at http://nrich.maths.org/7283.

Geogebra is an excellent, free, downloadable software package that links algebraic and geometric concepts in a way that develops and enriches both. It may be downloaded from the *Geogebra* website at http://www.geogebra.org/cms/.

You will also find instructions on the *Geogebra* website to get you going with the software. For more discussion and ideas, see:

Julie-Ann Edwards and Keith Jones: 'Linking geometry and algebra with Geogebra'. *Mathematics Teaching* **194**, January 2006.

A pack of 30 sets of **Tangram Tiles** may be obtained from Langton Info Services, at http://www.langtoninfo.co.uk/showitem.aspx?isbn=1564519406&loc=GBP. Alternatively, use the Tangram Tile outline on the CD to cut out your own.

Angle

a) What is an Angle?

An angle is a measure of turn. It is a *measure*, not a shape. Yet it is often not classified as part of the Measures curriculum. It is commonly introduced, first and foremost, as a property of two-dimensional shapes.

So – what is an angle? Can we draw an angle, and print the drawing on the page?

Well … no. We can't. An angle is a measure of *turn*. A turn is a movement. And we cannot draw a movement. At best, we can draw a representation of the movement – something like this, perhaps:

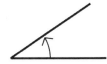

But very often, right from the start, we speak and write of an angle, and represent it, as if it were a relationship between a pair of lines. The crucial arrow, to show that the curved line represents a movement, is lost:

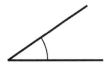

And in the case of a right angle, convention has done away with even the hint of movement conveyed by the arc:

So here again, the predominance of print over objects and models in the representation of a mathematical concept may undermine learners' understanding, and lead them to perceive an angle as a pair of straight lines rather than as a measure of turn. The kinaesthetic concept, which is all about movement, has been superseded by a static representation that is easier to print, but does nothing to convey the dynamic meaning of angle.

Introducing angle with Shape rather than with Measures may lead to a common misconception about the relative sizes of angles.

These two lines: are longer than these two lines:

so learners may not unreasonably
assume that this angle:

is greater than this angle:

They focus on the static, printed image of a pair of intersecting lines, rather than on the movement. The meaning of angle as a measure of turn, going from one direction to another, is lost.

In the Classroom – *Following Routes*

Learners can follow a series of instructions involving movement forward (and backwards) a number of steps, and clockwise or anti-clockwise turns. The turns may be expressed first as simple fractions of a turn – quarter-, half- and three-quarter turns, and then perhaps eighths of a turn. Later, learners may use an angle machine (see below) to help them to turn through other fractions of a turn or, eventually, angles expressed in degrees. Logo may be used to program a robot or a screen turtle to follow a path.

Activities (*activities* – not written exercises) that involve learners in turning either themselves or an object are essential to establish a foundation for the understanding of angle as a measure of turn. An angle machine, cut from card, provides a good model of angle as a measure of a turning movement (see Resource Sheet 8-1, *Angle Machine*). This can be marked off first in simple fractions of a turn – halves, quarters, thirds, sixths, and perhaps eighths or twelfths. Degrees can be introduced later as just another, smaller, fraction of a turn.

PowerPoint

PowerPoint 8-1, *What is an Angle?*, is designed to introduce the concept of angle as a measure of turn. It establishes the relationship between some key types of angle and the fractions of a turn that these involve.

Theme: Mathematical Language

Like other parts of the mathematics curriculum – and particularly the Geometry curriculum – Angle is littered with hard words for easy concepts. The 'mathematical' terms *acute*, *obtuse* and *reflex* are Latin: they just mean 'sharp', 'blunt' and 'reflected'.

b) Degrees

Learners may have been taught to use to use a protractor to measure angles in degrees, but this does not necessarily mean that they understand what a degree is. You might try an experiment with your learners. Ask them to show you *one degree*. You may find that many of them use their finger and thumb to show you a linear distance. It may be a very small distance – but it will identify a basic misconception that has been introduced and reinforced by our dependence on printed diagrams. These learners may not realise that a degree is just one, very small, fraction of a turn. Even if they understand the concept of a quarter turn and a half turn, and have practised turning through such fractions of a turn themselves, they may not relate the dynamic action of turning through an angle to the static printed diagrams in a mathematics textbook.

PowerPoint

PowerPoint 8-2, *Degrees*, introduces the concept of a degree as a measure of angle, and explains that a degree is just one – very small – fraction of a turn.

Theme: Making Links

If angle is thoroughly understood as a measure of turn then, here again, links may be made with other topics in different areas of the curriculum. A degree is just one particular example of a fraction of a turn. Degrees have been adopted by convention as the common units for the measure of angle, but they are not essentially different to other fractions of a turn. An analogue clock and a compass both rely on our ability to measure turn, although they use different units of measurement. On an analogue clock the hours, minutes and seconds are represented by the movement of the hands through twelfths and sixtieths of a whole turn, while a compass movement from, say, North to North East is one eighth of a whole turn. Linking angles firmly to the concept of fractions of a turn will help learners to understand both, and to use them in a range of contexts.

In the Classroom – *Growing Angles*

The angle machine (see Resource Sheet 8-1) can be used to show an angle increasing steadily in size. As it passes through 90° it goes from being *acute* (pointed) to being *obtuse* (blunt). Similarly the idea of a *straight* angle of 180°, which marks the barrier between *obtuse* (blunt) and *reflex* (reflected) angles, is much easier to grasp in the context of angle as a measure of turn.

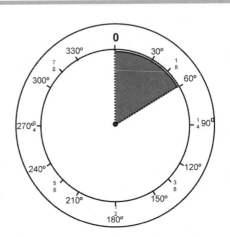

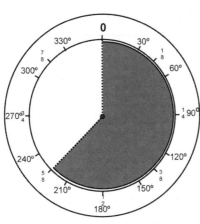

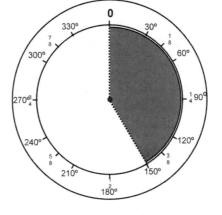

The dark centre-circle of the angle machine may be inserted on the plain side of the frame. This allows the teacher to show an angle 'growing' to a given size, which learners can estimate.

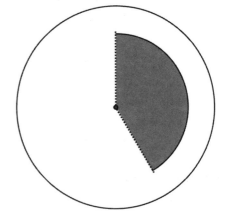

In the ~~Classroom~~ Playground – *360° Protractor and Compass*

A giant 360° protractor drawn and marked out at 10° or 30° intervals in the playground will encourage learners to think about angle as a measure of turn. Learners can stand in the middle, then turn themselves through a given angle. This kinaesthetic experience will be much more meaningful, and memorable, than measuring or 'drawing' static angles on paper.

If the protractor is oriented so that '0°' is to the north, and the points of the compass are added, then the link between angle as a measure of turn and compass directions will become clearer.

c) Angle Properties

If an angle is understood as a measure of turn, not as a static relationship between two straight lines, then many of its properties become easier to understand. For example, turning through a pair or a set of angles on a line involves turning through a half turn, or 180° – so angles on a line have a total measure of half a turn.

Similarly, turning through angles around a point involves turning through a whole turn, or 360° – so angles around a point have a total measure of one whole turn.

 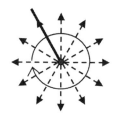

The angles in a grid of parallel lines form an interconnected whole, with only two sizes of angle,

 and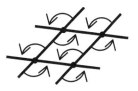

When the grid is squeezed, all the angles change together.

Theme: Mathematical Language – Angles in a Grid

Pairs of angles in a grid have special 'mathematical' names.

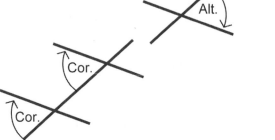

A pair of angles which are opposite each other on a pair of intersecting lines are *opposite*, which makes reasonably good sense.

The angles inside a Z-shape formed when a single line crosses a pair of parallel lines are called *alternate* angles.

A pair of angles sitting on a pair of parallel lines are said to be *corresponding* angles.

Yet more hard words for easy ideas!

In the Classroom – *Angles in a Grid*

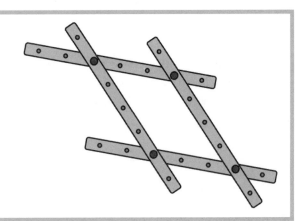

Learners can make a grid of plastic or card strips, joined together with split pin paper fasteners. As the model is expanded and contracted the pairs of opposite, alternate and corresponding angles increase or decrease together, always maintaining their equal measures.

d) Angles and Polygons – External Angles

Angle as a measure of turn is a dynamic, not a static, concept. It involves movement, not just a printed diagram. But what about the angles of a polygon? The angles of a triangle are static, aren't they? The triangle doesn't move, so nor do the angles!

Well, yes – the angles of a polygon can be seen as static. But what happens if we think about each angle as a turn?

When learners use an angle machine in the activity *Following Routes* they may walk around some simple polygons such as triangles or quadrilaterals. But 'walking round' a polygon is dynamic: as the learner reaches the end of a side they turn through the external angle of the polygon so that they face the direction of the next side.

For example, if you walk clockwise around a triangular flower bed you will keep turning right until you get back to where you started – and then you will have turned through one whole turn.

So if we regard the external angles of a polygon as fractions of a turn, we can see (just *see* – not calculate or memorise!) that the external angles of a polygon add up to one whole turn.

PowerPoint

PowerPoint 8-3, *External Angles*, uses a standard induction approach to explain dynamically why the external angles of a polygon always add up to a whole turn.

---

e) Angles and Polygons – Internal Angles

Turning through the external angles of a polygon is quite a familiar experience, even if we don't always recognise what we are doing. Walking around the edge of a rectangular swimming pool, for example, or around the outside of a building, involves turning through a series of external angles which, all together, will add up to one whole turn.

But what about turning through the *internal* angles of a polygon? That is not something we normally do, so it a bit more difficult to grasp.

If you walk around the triangle, but turn through the internal instead of the external angles, your path will look something like this:

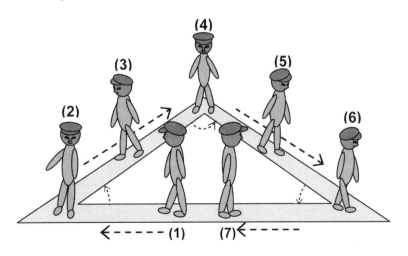

You start by walking forwards, along the first side of the triangle (1). But when you get to the first corner (2) you cannot turn right, or clockwise – that would take you through the external angle, as before. So instead you must turn left, or anti-clockwise, in order to turn through the internal angle. But this means that you will be facing the wrong way after you have made your turn, so you will have to walk backwards along the second side of the triangle (3). Then when you reach the second corner (4) you again turn left, or anti-clockwise, through the internal angle. Now you are facing the right direction, so you can walk forwards along the third side of the triangle (5). You carry on until you reach the third corner (6), but here again you must turn left, or anti-clockwise, through the internal angle, so you are facing the wrong way and have to walk backwards until you get back to your starting position. You have turned left, or anti-clockwise, through all three internal angles of the triangle, and in doing so you have turned through one half turn so you are facing the opposite direction to the one you started with. So the internal angles of a triangle add up to half a turn!

Theme: Mathematical Language – Supplementary and Complementary Angles

Angles which add up to a half turn give rise to another hard word for an easy concept: they are called *supplementary*. Angles which add up to a quarter turn are called *complementary*.

In the Classroom – *Internal Angles of a Polygon*

Draw a large triangle, then use a pencil or other pointer to 'walk' around it, turning through each **internal** angle as you come to it. Notice that whatever the shape of the triangle – equilateral, right-angled, isosceles or scalene – your pointer

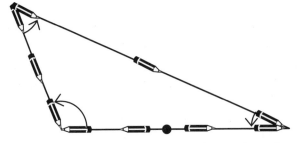

always ends up facing in the opposite direction to its starting position. The angles of a triangle *always* add up to half a turn.

When they have explored several different triangles, and are convinced that turning through their internal angles will always result in a half turn, learners can try turning through the internal angles of quadrilaterals. What do these add up

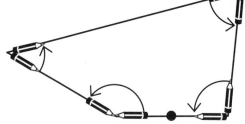

to? What happens when you turn through the internal angles of polygons with greater numbers of sides?

Learners can also try walking around a giant triangle and turning through its internal angles. They will need to make sure that they always turn anti-clockwise if they are walking clockwise round the triangle – otherwise they will be turning through the external angles instead!

In the Classroom – *Why 360 Degrees?*

Learners may be asked to find out *why* there are 360 degrees in a whole turn. Research into the history of mathematics should turn up a link to the Babylonians (see *Further Reading and Resources* below) – but mathematical reasons for choosing 360, as opposed to any other number, may also be discussed. 360 has a lot of factors, including 3, 4, 5 and 6, so the external and internal angles of an equilateral triangle, a square, and a regular pentagon and hexagon are all whole numbers of degrees. Learners might be asked what other regular polygons have angles which are whole numbers of degrees. Then they could consider what the effect would be of adopting a different convention – with, say, 100 degrees in a whole turn. Which regular polygons would have whole-number angles then?

PowerPoints

PowerPoint 8-4, *Internal Angles Part 1*, gives a dynamic representation of the process of turning through the internal angles of a triangle, and suggests that learners follow this up by exploring the process with polygons with greater numbers of sides.

PowerPoint 8-5, *Internal Angles Part 2*, suggests one way to think about the relationship between the number of sides in the polygons and the number of whole and half turns in its internal angles.

Angle – Teaching Points

■ Angle should be taught as a *measure*, not just as a property of shapes.

■ The concept of angle as a measure of turn is often lost in static images on the printed page.

■ Focusing on static angles can lead to misconceptions.

■ Here again, learners need visual and kinaesthetic 'pictures in the mind' that they can use as a basis for their mathematical thinking.

■ Activities that involve learners moving an object or themselves through common fractions of a turn will help them to recognise angle as a measure of turn.

■ Degrees may be introduced as just another example of a fraction of a turn.

■ Manipulating models will help learners to see the relationships between the angles on a grid.

■ Angles in polygons can be viewed dynamically, as a fraction of a turn.

Resources on the CD

Mathematical PowerPoints

> PP 8-1 *What is an Angle?*
>
> PP 8-2 *Degrees*
>
> PP 8-3 *External Angles*
>
> PP 8-4 *Internal Angles Part 1*
>
> PP 8-5 *Internal Angles Part 2*

Resource Sheet

> RS 8-1 *Angle Machine*

Further Reading and Resources

Logo is a programming language that allows learners to explore many aspects of angle and shape, and to develop their understanding in an active, engaging and meaningful way. A version of Logo may be downloaded free from Softronics, Inc, at http://www.softronix.com/.

Peter Smith of Sheffield Hallam University has written a useful set of booklets to support teachers and learners working with Logo. These may be downloaded from the website of the Association of Teachers of Mathematics, at http://www.atm.org.uk/resources/logo.html.

To find out more about the background and philosophy of Logo, read: Seymour Papert, 1996: 'An Exploration in the Space of Mathematics Educations'. *International Journal of Computers for Mathematical Learning*, Vol. 1, No. 1, pp. 95–123, available at: http://www.papert.org/articles/AnExplorationintheSpaceofMathematicsEducations.html.

An internet search will turn up a lot of information about how we have ended up with **360 degrees** in a whole turn. For example, visit http://www.wikipedia.org/ and search for 'Degree (angle)'.

CHAPTER 9

Perimeter, Area and Volume

Some key concepts

- A *perimeter* is a distance. An *area* may be thought of as 'an amount of flatness'.

- A parallelogram can be sheared back into a rectangle with the same area.
  A triangle can be sheared back into a right-angled triangle with the same area.

- A container has a *capacity*. A solid has a *volume*.

- A cubic container measuring 10cm by 10cm by 10cm has a capacity of 1 litre. It will hold 1 litre of water, which weighs 1 kilogram.

---

a) Vocabulary

School mathematics is steeped in hard words. Indeed, language is a theme that crops up repeatedly throughout this book. But nowhere is it more evident than in geometry and measures. Mathematical language may present a major hurdle to learners who could otherwise fly with the ideas and images of shape and space, causing them instead to crash on the mass of mathematical jargon. *Kilogram, perimeter, pentagon* … these are all hard words, although they refer to quite straightforward ideas.

It is worth spending time making as much sense as possible out of the jargon, demystifying it wherever you can. *Pentagon*, for example, is simply the Greek for *five sides*. Talking in Greek is no more mathematically correct than talking in English – so *pentagon* is not a more mathematical term than *five sides*. Our use of Greek and Latin in the mathematics classroom is just a historical accident – and it is not helpful to learners who may find it harder to remember the new words than to understand what they mean in the first place.

Learners need to acquire a lot of mathematical jargon in order to achieve under our curriculum and assessment structure. However, it is important always to keep a clear distinction between the mathematical concepts that need to be understood, and the vocabulary used to describe them. So, for example, learners may identify pairs of shapes that are exactly the same, and others that are the same shape but different sizes, long before they learn the 'mathematical' terms *congruent* and *similar*. Some learners may succeed in such mathematical activities but struggle to get started in vocabulary-heavy tasks. Mathematical terminology may form a barrier for these learners, and they are likely to engage with the subject better if they are presented with some activities that do not present linguistic hurdles.

Theme: Mathematical Language – Vocabulary Posters and Movements

Posters headed *Hard Words, Easy Ideas* illustrating the concepts and offering simple, illustrated translations of so-called 'mathematical' (usually Latin or Greek) terms may help learners to understand, and so to remember, the words they need.

Some learners may also find it helpful to associate words with movements. If you are fortunate enough to have a hearing impaired learner who uses Sign in the classroom then they may be willing to demonstrate some of the signs they use for mathematical terms (see *Further Reading and Resources* below for a CD of mathematical signs). These are often far more meaningful than the accepted spoken and written words. Alternatively, learners might create their own movements which convey the meanings of mathematical terms that they find hard to remember, and practise saying the words while carrying out the movements.

---

b) Area and Perimeter

Two concepts that are often introduced together are *area* and *perimeter*. Learners spend time drawing shapes on squared paper, and counting and recording the number of squares used (the area), and the number of units around the edge (the perimeter). But this approach focuses on the numbers – and to a visual and kinaesthetic thinker one number may be very like another, so *area* and *perimeter* are likely to get muddled.

But area and perimeter are quite different concepts. *Perimeter* is fairly straightforward. It is the distance around a shape. I can walk around the perimeter of a large shape, or trace my pencil around the perimeter of a smaller one – so I can see and feel what a perimeter is. But *area* is more difficult to understand. It may be thought of as 'an amount of flatness'.

Theme: Mathematical Language – Area and Perimeter

The 'mathematical' terms *area* and *perimeter* may become easier to remember if they are associated with appropriate movements.

Area may be thought of as a 'measure of flatness'. A common sign for area is a hand held flat above the table, and moved round in a horizontal plane as if to smooth the air underneath.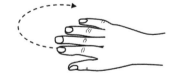

A *perimeter* is the distance around a shape. The common sign for this uses both hands. The forefinger of the left hand is held up, and then a roughly square path is sketched out in the air with the forefinger of the right hand.

In the Classroom – *Tiles and Sticks*

Activities that relate *area* and *perimeter* to different materials may provide a firmer foundation than mere counting for the development of these concepts. Square tiles, which can be picked up and moved around, provide a better starting point for area than drawn squares. A set of sticks that are the same length as the edge of a tile provide a model of the perimeter. The challenge may then be set to surround a given number of tiles with different numbers of sticks, or to fill different spaces, each surrounded by a given number of sticks, with different numbers of tiles. This is mathematically equivalent to finding sets of shapes with the same area but different perimeters, or the same perimeter but different areas – but it focuses on the common values of the area or the perimeter, not on the words.

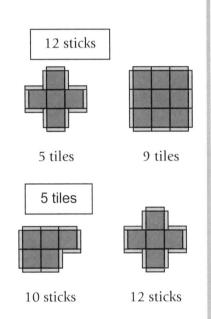

This is certainly not a new type of activity. Shapes made with squares joined together edge-to-edge are called *polyominoes* – like *dominoes*, which are made with two squares, but with 'many' (*poly*) instead of 'two'. Simply finding lots of different polyominoes made with different numbers of square tiles is a valuable activity in itself. Finding their areas and perimeters is a natural development. But using square tiles and unit sticks will help learners to focus distinctly on the two different measures, area and perimeter. In time they may well switch to the conventional drawings on squared paper – but the memory and feel of the square tiles and the sticks will help them to keep sight of the meaning of the different measures they are using.

PowerPoint

PowerPoint 9-1, *Tangram Areas*, offers a context in which learners may explore and quantify the areas of a set of shapes without using any formulas. Outlines for sets of Tangram Tiles are also on the CD in Resource Sheet 7-1, *Tangram Tiles*.

c) Models for Formulas

School mathematics is riddled with 'procedures', which learners may be expected to learn, remember and apply. Geometry and Measures are as badly affected in this respect as any other area of the curriculum. Test and examination papers commonly include a Formula Sheet, in which all the learner's understanding of the concepts of area and volume are reduced to a set of rules. Even when this sheet is not provided learners may still be taught the formulas by rote, rather than developing an understanding of the mathematics that underlies them. Then, of course, they forget them.

So here again, learners who think more easily in pictures than in words and symbols need 'models to think with'. The models make sense, so they are memorable – unlike the formulas, which are eminently forgettable. And having remembered the relevant model, the 'picture in the mind', the learner can work out the formula they need for the problem they are working on.

d) Areas of Straight-Sided Shapes

The first formula learners are likely to meet is for the area of a rectangle. They start by finding the areas of small rectangles by counting squares – that is, by yet more sequential recitation of disconnected number words. This follows logically from the standard introduction to Number, relying heavily on counting, that was discussed in Chapter 2, but it is less helpful for learners who see the whole picture at once. On the other hand, visualising a rectangle, and finding its area, lies at the heart of the area model of multiplication discussed in Chapter 3. Learners who see the calculation 3 × 4, for example, as

have no need of a formula. They already understand the relationship between the edge lengths and the area of a rectangle on which the formula is based.

The area of a parallelogram can be worked out directly from the area of a rectangle. The parallelogram can be cut into pieces, then reconstructed into a rectangle.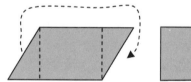

Alternatively, a possibly more memorable model can be made from a stack of cards, such as playing cards or off-cuts from a print shop, formed into a block.

An elastic band holds the stack together, but allows it to be sheared one way or the other. The front face of the stack, which was a rectangle, is transformed by the shearing into a parallelogram.

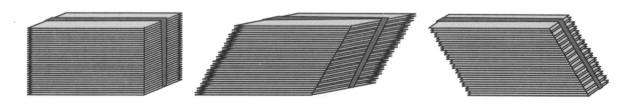

The top card in the stack has not been raised or lowered, it has only been sheared to the right or the left – so the height of the model has not changed. The bottom card has not moved at all, so the parallelogram has the same base and the same height as the original rectangle. It also has the same area, since no cards have been added or removed. With this kinaesthetic and visual 'picture in the mind' on which to base their thinking, learners can see how any parallelogram can be sheared back into a rectangle with the same base, height and area.

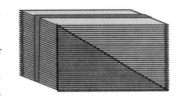

Using the same model, a diagonal line and some shading drawn on the other side of the stack will help learners to perceive a right-angled triangle as half of a rectangle. Any other triangle can then be seen as a shearing of a right-angled triangle with the same base length, height and area.

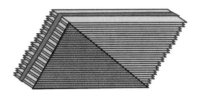

This 'model to think with' can be applied to any parallelogram or triangle, so that the learner can mentally transform the figure on the page back into a rectangle or right-angled triangle. Then the base and height can be identified easily, and so its area may be found. There is no need for a formula: the process is visual and kinaesthetic, not symbolic.

PowerPoint

PowerPoint 9-2, *Areas of Straight-Sided Shapes*, shows how to find the area of a parallelogram or a triangle by first shearing it so that it has a right angle, and then basing the calculations on the area of the resulting rectangle.

---

e) Capacity and Volume

We have seen that *area* can be thought of as 'an amount of flatness'. It is a strictly two-dimensional concept. *Capacity* and *volume*, on the other hand, are three-dimensional. But our world is three-dimensional, so these concepts may actually be easier to understand.

Capacity may be the best place to start. A capacity relates to a particular container, and it tells you how much that container can hold. This idea may be established using informal measures, such as the number of small cups-full that are needed to fill a big jug.

Volume, on the other hand, is the amount of 'stuff' that is needed to make a solid. Activities which involve building up cuboids a layer at a time out of cubic-centimetre cubes to find their volumes are commonly used to introduce a more formal measure of volume. This is a good practical approach, and it may be extended in due course to other solids – but it is important to emphasise that the volume relates to the whole block of cubes, not to an empty container. An empty carton has a capacity – but it is empty, so its only 'volume' is the volume of plastic or cardboard of which it is composed. But if we fill the carton with water then that water will have a volume – a volume that is equal to the capacity of the container.

So how can we tie up the capacity of the container with the volume of its contents? Well, litres are common in everyday life, and children will have come across containers of milk, juice, cooking oil and so forth with capacities given in litres. And the really interesting thing about a litre of water is that it will exactly fill a cubic container that measures 10cm by 10cm by 10cm – so one litre of anything has a volume of 1000 cubic centimetres. And what is more, one litre of water weighs (has a mass of) one kilogram.

In the Classroom – *Litres and Cubic Centimetres*

Learners can find the capacity of a 10cm by 10cm by 10cm cube by filling it up, then transferring the contents into a standard litre measure. This gives us the really useful fact that a litre has a volume of 1000 cubic centimetres.

Unfortunately, making a cube that will actually hold a litre of water is tricky. If you make it out of card it just gets soggy, and other materials are difficult to seal so the cube is likely to leak. It is probably better to rely on a commercially-produced cube with a capacity of a litre – a quick search on the internet will suggest several suppliers (see *Further Reading and Resources* below). Alternatively, the 10cm by 10cm by 10cm cube can be made out of card and then filled with a dry substance such as rice or sand which can be transferred into the litre measure.

Theme: Making Links – Decimal Numbers and Metric Measures

There is obviously a close link between decimal numbers and metric measures. Learners whose understanding of decimal numbers is firmly embedded in the *cubes → sticks → slabs → cubes* cycle discussed in Chapter 4, *Place Value and Decimals*, will readily grasp the relationship between millilitres (cubic centimetres) and litres (10cm by 10cm by 10cm cubes), using the same 'model to think with'.

Theme: Language – Metric Measures

The system of metric measures has the advantage that it is consistent, so there are not, in fact, very many new words to learn. The word *kilo*, for example, just means a *thousand*, whether it be a *kilo-gram*, a *kilo-metre*, or a *kilo-litre*. Learners may be invited to invent their own uses of *kilo* – so a *kilo-tree*, for instance, might be a wood with a thousand trees, or a *kilo-book*, a library with a thousand books. What could we mean by a *kilo-learner*, or a *kilo-smile*?

Perimeter, Area and Volume – Teaching Points

- Diagrams and models form the basis of Geometry and Measures, but the static limitations of the printed page often dominate the curriculum.

- 'Mathematical' vocabulary often hides, instead of revealing, meaning.

- Meaningful movements, such as those used in signing, may help learners to recall some mathematical terms.

- *Area* and *perimeter* are often confused. The distinction between area and perimeter can be established more firmly with the use of a different material to represent each measure.

- Key concepts are often reduced to a set of formulas and lost in static images on the printed page.

- Learners who think more easily in pictures than in words and symbols struggle to remember formulas. A kinaesthetic and visual 'picture in the mind' is more meaningful, and therefore more memorable.

- The words used in the metric measures system – kilo, centi, milli – may be explored and understood across a range of contexts.

Resources on the CD

Mathematical PowerPoints

   PP 9-1 *Tangram Areas*

   PP 9-2 *Areas of Straight-Sided Shapes*

Further Reading and Resources

A CD showing signs for a wide range of mathematical terms, *Signs for Maths*, is available from Microbooks Ltd, at http://www.microbooks.org/product/bsl-british-sign-language/signs-for-maths.html. These may be useful for any learner who finds meaningful movements easier to remember than arbitrary words.

A set of plastic containers, including a **litre cube** and three other shapes each with a capacity of one litre, may be obtained from Philip Harris at http://www.philipharris.co.uk/product/B8A74249.

Circles and Time

Some key concepts

- π is a ratio. π is the number of times I would have to walk straight across a circle (the *diameter*) in order to go the same distance as someone walking all the way round it (the *circumference*).

- π is a bit more than 3, so the circumference of a circle is a bit more than 3 times the diameter.

- A circle may be opened out into a triangle whose base is the circumference, and whose height is the radius. The area of the triangle (half its base times its height) is the same as the area of the circle (half its circumference times its radius).

- We measure time with a range of inter-locking cycles. An analogue clock shows the relationship between minutes and hours. We can think about the other cycles in the same way.

---

a) Circles and π

We saw in Chapter 9, *Perimeter, Area and Volume*, how learners may be expected to just remember and use formulas, with little understanding of where they come from or why they work. The formulas for the area and circumference of a circle are often treated in this way, and they are probably the most consistently confused in the mathematics curriculum. There are few combinations of '2', '*r*', '*r²*', 'π' and 'π^2' that do not turn up, at one time or another, masquerading as 'formulas' in the piles of exercise books from learners who are struggling with the dimensions of a circle.

The first problem is π. What is π? Is it a number? Is it 3.14159 …, or whatever?

Well – not exactly. It is a ratio. π is the number of times I would have to walk across a circle in order to go the same distance as someone walking all the way round it.

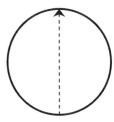
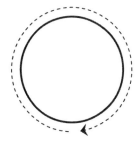

How many times *straight across* is the same as *all the way round?*

Using this kinaesthetic, movement-based approach, it is not hard to see that the number of times must be greater than 2. 2 would take me straight across and straight back, with no allowance made for the curved nature of the path around the edge of the circle.

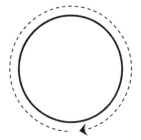
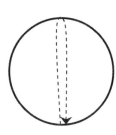

All the way round is more than *there and back.*
So π is more than 2.

But it cannot be as much as 4, because 4 times the distance straight across the middle of the circle would take me along the edge of a square which surrounds the circle. I would be walking further than the person going right round the edge of the circle, because she would be cutting the corners of my square.

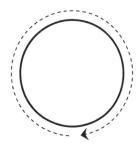
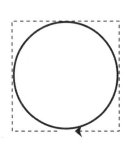

Round the circle is less than *round the square.*
So π is less than 4.

So π must be more than 2 but less than 4. As a first approximation, π is 3.

In fact, π is just a little bit more than 3. We can see this by thinking about a regular hexagon, made up of equilateral triangles.

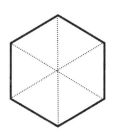

Walking right round the hexagon would take me along six triangle edge-lengths. This is *exactly* 3 times the distance straight across the middle.

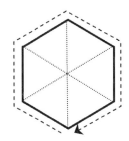
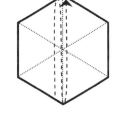

The distance
right round the hexagon   is exactly   3 times the distance
straight across the middle.

A circle that just fits around the hexagon will have the same distance straight across the middle as the hexagon.

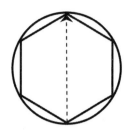

But the distance round the circle is a little bit more than the distance round the hexagon. So it is a little bit more than 3 times the distance straight across the middle. So π is a little bit more than 3.

π relates the distance all the way round a circle to the distance straight across it. It relates the *circumference* to the *diameter*, to use the popular (among mathematicians) jargon. The circumference is a little bit more than 3 times the diameter. This number, 'a little more than 3', is π. So the circumference is π times the diameter.

But that can create another confusion. π is defined in terms of the circumference and the *diameter* – the distance around the circle, and the distance *all* the way across. But the standard formulas for the circumference and area of a circle, $C = 2\pi r$, and $A = \pi r^2$, are expressed in terms of the circumference and the *radius*. This is the distance *half* way across the circle, not *all* the way. Learners need to understand clearly the difference between these two distances – which is easy if they are part of a picture, on paper or in the mind, but much more difficult if they are just squiggles on the page.

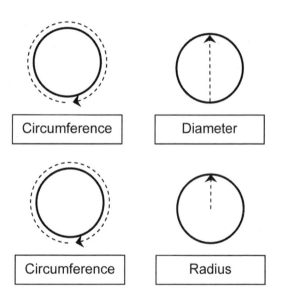

So we can see – literally *see* if we draw or imagine a circle that just fits around a regular hexagon – that the circumference of a circle is 3 and a bit, or π, times the diameter. This is the same as π times double the radius, so $C = \pi \times 2r$, or $2\pi r$. The formula can be taken directly out of the 'picture in the mind': there is no need to memorise it.

PowerPoint

PowerPoint 10-1, *Circumference of a Circle*, will help learners to establish the 'picture in the mind' that they need so that they can understand *why* the distance all the way round a circle is a little bit more than 3 times the distance straight across the middle.

---

b) The Area of a Circle

Now that we have a way to visualise – to just *see* – that the circumference of a circle is π times the diameter, we are ready to think about its area. This needs a different 'model to think with'. First, we imagine a circle that is sliced from the top to the centre, and then opened out into a wide, low triangle.

circumference

The area of the circle is the same as the area of the triangle.

The base of the triangle is the circumference of the circle.

The height of the triangle is the radius of the circle.

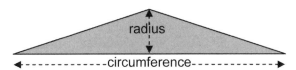
radius
circumference

The area of any triangle is half its base times its height. So the area of this circle-turned-triangle is half the circumference times the radius.

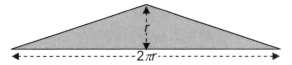
r
$2\pi r$

In symbols, the area of the circle (*or* of the triangle) is ½ × 2πr × r, or πr².

Here again, the aim of the models and images is to establish visual and kinaesthetic 'pictures in the mind' that learners can recall later, and use not to *remember* the formulas, but rather to *reconstruct* them when they are needed.

In the Classroom – *Area of a Circle*

A model may be made, consisting of a series of rings of large beads threaded on string that can be opened out to form a triangle.

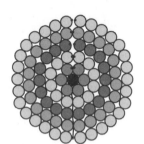

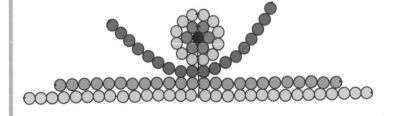

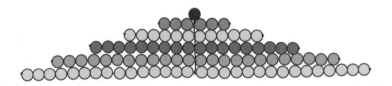

Alternatively, a set of magnetic marbles (see *Further Reading and Resources* below) may be arranged into a circle, starting from the centre and building out one ring at a time. With care and a little practice, this can be opened out to form the triangle.

PowerPoint

PowerPoint 10-2, *Area of a Circle*, offers a dynamic image of a circle of beads opening out to form a triangle which can be sheared so that its area can be found.

Theme: Making Links – Volumes of Cuboids, Prisms and Cylinders

Learners may have built up an understanding of the volume of a cuboid by placing several rectangular layers of cubic centimetre cubes one on top of another, and then finding the total number of cubes in the cuboid. This image of 'layering' may be extended to other prisms and to cylinders. For example, the coloured screw top from a plastic milk bottle is (more or less) cylindrical, and it has a diameter of (roughly) 4 centimetres and a height of (about) 1 centimetre. The (approximate) capacity of one of these bottle tops may be found by filling it with water and measuring the water with an ordinary kitchen measuring spoon, or it may be calculated. Either way, it will be about 12 ½ cubic centimetres.

Several of these bottle tops may be piled up one on top of another to make a bigger cylinder.

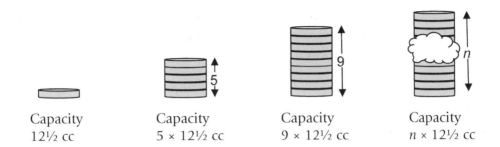

Capacity	Capacity	Capacity	Capacity
12½ cc	5 × 12½ cc	9 × 12½ cc	n × 12½ cc

The volume of a 'tower' of n small cylinders will always be n times as much as the volume of one small cylinder. This image will help learners to understand where the *times height* comes from in the formula for the volume of a cylinder or prism,

volume = base area times height

c) Time

Time is one of the most difficult topics that we have to teach. But it is also one of the most useful and relevant. It may not be obvious to the learner why she needs to understand fractions, or the angles of a triangle, or how to solve an equation, or whatever. But time – well, yes, we use it every day. So why is it such a challenge for many of our learners?

One reason may be that our experience of time is so unlike the way we represent and work with it. We treat time as if it were additive – so that two years is twice as long as one year and three years is half as long again. That may be objectively true, but it is not how we experience it subjectively. To a child of ten, 'half his life' is five years. He can only dimly remember what he was doing, what it felt like to be himself, five years ago. But to a woman of fifty, 'half her life' is twenty-five years. She may well have a clearer memory of being twenty-five than the ten-year-old has of being five. In a very real sense, the fifty-year-old's experience of twenty-five years is equivalent to, or possibly even shorter than, the ten-year-old's experience of five years.

Furthermore, even in the short term, time as we experience it really does not run at a steady pace. It slows down or speeds up in startling fashion, depending on what we are doing and how we are feeling. So *The minutes crawled past as we waited anxiously for news*; but *The day flashed by in a whirl of excitement!* The small hours of the morning pass without our even being aware of them if we are asleep – but they may drag interminably if we are restless and awake. What they rarely do is to pass at the same rate as the hours of, say, an ordinary afternoon.

But if we were to acknowledge that time passes at different rates at different times for each of us then we would have no way of measuring it. We could not identify a particular point in time, or all agree to do something for a particular length of time. So instead we pretend that an hour is an hour is an hour … although we all know perfectly well, if we stop and think about it, that it is not.

Another game we play is to pretend that our division of time into years, months, weeks and days is fixed by natural phenomena and is absolute. But in reality, of course, all our complicated systems for measuring time are based on a series of approximations. Using a Gregorian calendar we say that there are 365 days in a year (usually); twelve months in a year (that is true, but the months are different sizes); four weeks in a month (that only applies to February, actually – and not always then). It is true that there are seven days in a week, but none of the sums work: there are not exactly fifty-two weeks in a year.

So what can we do to help learners to find their way through all these confusing inaccuracies and counter-intuitive conventions? There is no magic wand, but it may be a good start to mention the time at frequent intervals throughout the day. Have a large, clear analogue clock with easy-to-read numbers on permanent display in the classroom, and see who can spot when the long hand is pointing upwards. Tell the learners that it is whatever o'clock at this time. When that idea is firmly established, draw attention to the long hand between the 'o'clock' times. Stop at a time when it is pointing straight down and ask what is happening. In this way you can begin to build up the connection between the fractions of an hour and fractions of a turn. If you are lucky someone may suggest 'three quarters past ten' or 'a third to two'. There is nothing wrong with these as ways of expressing particular times, and any learner who comes up with them has clearly grasped the concept.

Theme: Making Links – Clocks, Angles and Fractions of a Turn

An analogue clock is a very useful model for a number of things, including the addition of fractions and the concept of angle, but perhaps its most significant role is to do what it was designed for in the first place: to represent time. The clock represents time as a set of interconnected cycles. The minute hand goes round twelve times faster than the hour hand, so one complete cycle of the hour hand over a period of twelve hours requires twelve cycles of the minute hand. Another way of saying this is that we measure hours in whole turns with the minute hand, but we measure them in twelfths of a turn with the hour hand. This is a key idea, and it is one that may be demonstrated well with the learners themselves in the classroom activity below, *Clock Cycles*.

In the Classroom – *Clock Cycles*

Draw a large circle on the floor or in the playground, and mark it off into twelve sections numbered 1 to 12 like a clock face. Ask one learner to be the hour hand, and another to be the minute hand. Explain that they are going to show what happens in one hour on the clock. Both hands start at 12 at the 'top' of the clock. The hour hand should stand just inside the circle and the minute hand just outside because the hour hand is normally shorter than the minute hand. Then while the minute hand walks quickly round the whole circle, the hour hand moves very slowly from the 12 to the 1, watching where the minute hand has got to and aiming to arrive at 1 just as the minute hand gets back to 12. Then the two hands can show another hour, and another – although the minute hand may get worn out and need to be replaced!

An old geared clock that will allow you to demonstrate how the hour hand moves when the minute hand is moved will be very useful if you can get hold of one. But please don't use an ungeared model whose hands can be moved independently! It is the relationship between the movement of the two hands that is crucial here – and moving one hand while the other stays still could undermine this key understanding.

The clock face is divided into sixty little angles – remember, angle is a measure of turn, so these are sixtieths of a turn. These sixtieths are subdivided into twelve sets of five, giving us a set of twelfths of a turn around the clock face. These twelfths of a turn are labelled 1 to 12, rather than 5, 10, 15 and so forth, which is fine for the hours but confusing for the minutes. But when the learners are ready to move on from 'fractions of a turn' (*half past; quarter to*; perhaps *one third past; one sixth to*) to 'minutes past' or 'minutes to' the hour, the minutes may be added on sticky labels all around the outside of the clock face.

Time goes by in cycles which are well-represented on a clock face, but timetables are usually laid out in a linear format. But there is no need for this: writing the various events that occur through the day around a clock gives a clearer picture of what time actually means. The school day fits conveniently onto one clock face, so a week's timetable may be represented on a series of five clock faces. Then, when these five images have been built up and experienced a number of times, perhaps over half a term, the different events – 'school starts', 'maths lesson', 'break', 'dinner', and so forth – may be copied across onto a more conventional timetable layout, with one row or one column for each day of the week. But leave the clock faces up on display as well, so that learners can think about the relationship between the times on the school timetable and the times displayed on the clocks.

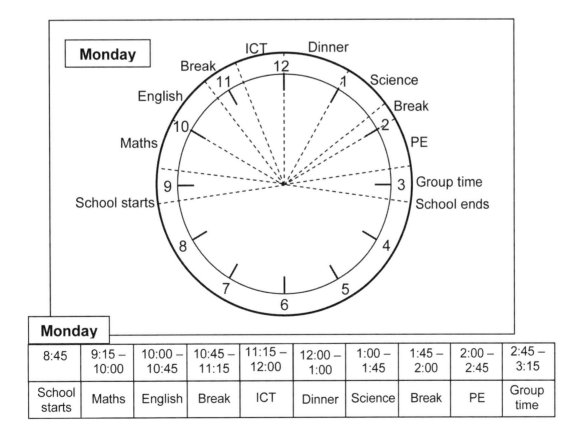

Monday

8:45	9:15 – 10:00	10:00 – 10:45	10:45 – 11:15	11:15 – 12:00	12:00 – 1:00	1:00 – 1:45	1:45 – 2:00	2:00 – 2:45	2:45 – 3:15
School starts	Maths	English	Break	ICT	Dinner	Science	Break	PE	Group time

In the Classroom – *Cyclic Weeks, Months and Years*

We commonly use clocks to represent the cycle of time through the day. We rarely use the same approach to represent the days of a week. But weeks, too, are cyclic: Monday always comes after Sunday and it is followed by Tuesday every week. Similarly, the months of the year are cyclic – they always run from January through to December. The days of a month are more or less cyclic – they all start with the 1st, although they do not all have a 29th, 30th, and 31st day.

See Resource Sheet 10-1, *Cyclic Calendar*, for a set of three cyclic charts, each with a moveable pointer to show the day of the week, the day of the month, and the month of the year. These may be used to represent the date each day in a way that, unlike a conventional calendar, really does convey the cyclic nature of time.

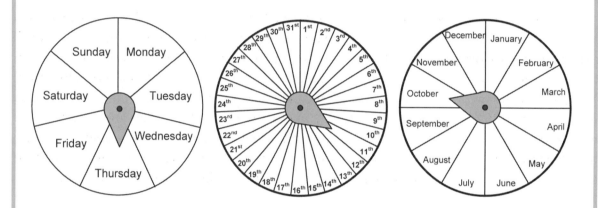

Cyclic Calendar showing *Thursday, 11th October*

Circles and Time – Teaching Points

- Learners' understanding of π should be based on the relationship between the diameter and the circumference of a circle.

- The formulas for the circumference and area of a circle can be taken directly out of the models and the 'pictures in the mind'. They should be understood, not memorised.

- Time is measured as if it passed at a constant rate, but in our experience it seems to slow down and speed up.

- The 'cycles' of time are presented as if they were regular, but all our measurements are based on approximations.

Resources on the CD

Mathematical PowerPoints

> PP 10-1 *Circumference of a Circle*

> PP 10-2 *Area of a Circle*

Resource Sheet

> RS 10-1 *Cyclic Calendar*

Further Reading and Resources

Magnetic marbles, used to make the Area of a Circle model, may be obtained from Rapid at http://www.rapidonline.com/Education/Tub-of-100-Magnetic-Marbles-06-6296.

Data Handling

Some key concepts

- We can collect data and represent each data point in different ways.

- A whole data set can be displayed with different sorts of graphical representation.

- The mode and median of a set of data can be found by arranging and comparing the data points.

- The mean of a set of data is just 'what it would be if all the data values were equal'.

- Percentages can be useful to compare proportions, but they may disguise sample sizes that are too small to be meaningful.

---

a) Seeing the Data

Data handling has a rather special place in the school mathematics curriculum. It is generally agreed that an understanding of statistics and their representation is essential in a literate and numerate society, if only to help us to distinguish the 'damn lies' from the 'statistics' in political speeches and newspaper articles. But data handling is a relative newcomer to the school curriculum, and this may be why it is often approached in a different way to the rest of mathematics. Statistics, after all, have to be about something – and that 'something' may affect the way the subject is presented and discussed. It may provide a context for the lists and tables of figures, and this can help to give them some meaning. Mathematics textbook writers and examiners are often happy enough to require learners to do a calculation, or to find a length or an angle in an abstract diagram, with no context. But if learners are asked to draw a bar chart, or to find the mean of a set of figures, then this must be in order to represent and process some data – and that data is likely to have a context. It may even relate to observations or results that the learners themselves have collected. Generally speaking, school mathematics exercises in data handling are more likely than those in other areas of the curriculum to be in context.

The raw data itself – the lists of figures and tables – can be quite daunting. But many school data-handling activities involve data that is summarised and represented in a range of graphical forms, and this can make the topic more meaningful to learners who think more easily in pictures than in numbers and symbols. For example, the same information about a group of learners who are members of a dance and a music club might be shown in two forms – on a table, and in a Venn Diagram.

Music only	Dance only	Both
11	8	4

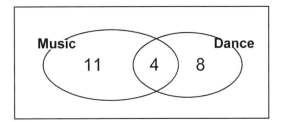

The diagram brings out the relationships between the figures in a way that the simple table cannot do. The total group of dancers, for example, is shown in the right hand loop, while the dancers who are also members of the music club are shown in the middle where the two loops overlap. The position of the figures on the diagram mirrors the positions of the learners they represent in the two groups.

A long list of figures may convey little in itself, but even a simple bar chart can allow us to take in the overall shape of the data at a glance. For example, this table shows the number of goals scored by a team in each of twelve matches in one season.

Match	1st	2nd	3rd	4th	5th	6th	7th	8th	9th	10th	11th	12th
Goals	2	0	3	2	3	2	2	0	4	1	3	2

This raw data can be collected into a frequency table, to show how often the team scored 0, 1, 2, 3 or 4 goals.

Number of goals	0	1	2	3	4
Number of matches	2	1	5	3	1

But this table still presents a bewildering array of figures. The same information can be presented more graphically in a bar chart.

The bar chart gives an overall picture of the data. For example, it enables us to see at once, with no need for any computation, that in more than half of the matches the team scored two or three goals. Graphical representations like these can help learners to get beyond the detail of the specific figures to look at their overall shape, and the relationships between the different parts. This will enable them to grasp the whole pattern, without being distracted and possibly confused by the individual values that make up the total data set.

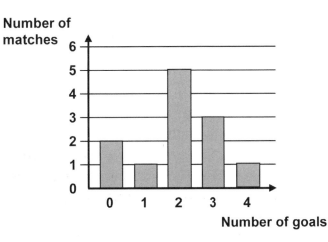

b) Using Non-numerical Data

Many data-handling activities require learners to work with a lot of numbers. Data sets are often composed solely of numbers, sometimes in large collections. For those learners who think more easily in pictures and movements the numbers may get in the way of their understanding of key concepts.

An alternative approach is to use the learners themselves as the starting point for work on data handling. The data to be processed is not collected as sets of figures. Instead, the learners form the 'data points' to be 'processed'.

In the Classroom – *Sorting Learners*

The learners themselves can provide a good entry point for work on sorting diagrams. They may be physically arranged on a giant sorting diagram marked out on the floor, with the cells labelled with two different pairs of mutually exclusive criteria – for example, *Girls* and *Boys*, and *Left-handed* and *Right-handed*.

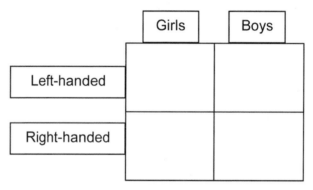

This sort, or a similar one on a Venn diagram, may be recorded on paper using a sticky label to represent each learner.

In the Classroom – *Scattered Learners*

Another type of representation in which the learners can provide the data points directly is a scatter graph.

Prepare a large grid with the axes labelled with the two measures whose relationship is to be graphed. For instance, the scatter graph might show two body measurements, such as *height* and *hand span*, or it might show *distance travelled to school* against *time taken*.

Each learner takes a sticky label, such as a small post-it note, writes their initials on the label, and sticks it in the correct position on the scatter graph. If this is done bit by bit, with different groups of learners adding their labels one after another, the overall pattern of the relationship between the two sets of data will emerge gradually. Each learner's identity with one particular point on the scatter graph – 'That label there is *me*!' – will help them to understand the whole diagram as a collection of individual data points, without losing sight of the overall shape of the data. With this approach there are no lists of figures to be processed. Rather, the graph is built up directly from the data.

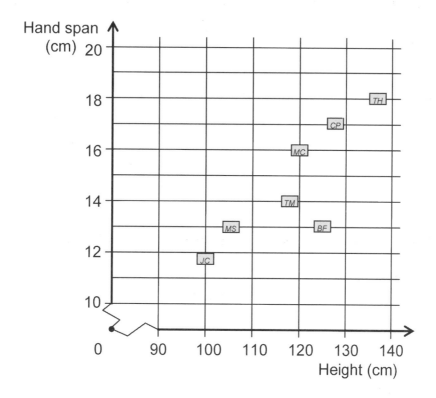

Plotting different measures against each other will help learners to recognise the concepts of strong, weak and no correlation. Either of the graphs described above, for example, is likely to produce some degree of positive correlation – taller learners are more likely to have a larger hand span than shorter, and learners who travel further are likely to take longer. On the other hand, *hand span* is not likely to correlate with *distance travelled to school*, and a plotting of these two factors may show the lack of relationship clearly.

Once they have grasped the concept of a scatter graph the learners themselves may suggest other properties of data sets that can be graphed against one another. When each point on a scatter graph represents a particular learner the meaning of the statistics and their representation will become clearer.

Another non-numerical approach to data collection and processing builds on the learners' work with shapes. The mathematical properties of shapes may be used as a basis for sorting and classifying activities which provide good opportunities for data representation without any need for numbers.

Theme: Making Links – Symmetry Properties and Sorting Diagrams

Different kinds of sorting diagrams, such as Carroll or Venn diagrams, may be created using a set of shapes. Activities like these, which bypass the numbers and enable learners to build up a graph or a diagram directly as the data is collected, will help them to understand the principles of data handling without having to worry about the figures.

	Line of symmetry	No line of symmetry
4 squares or fewer		
More than 4 squares		

Theme: Making Links – Area and Perimeter Scatter Graph

A scatter graph may be used to develop learners' understanding of the relationship between area and perimeter. Shapes made with different numbers of squares (*polyominoes*) may be cut out, and stuck onto a large graph with *Area* along the *x*-axis and *Perimeter* along the *y*-axis.

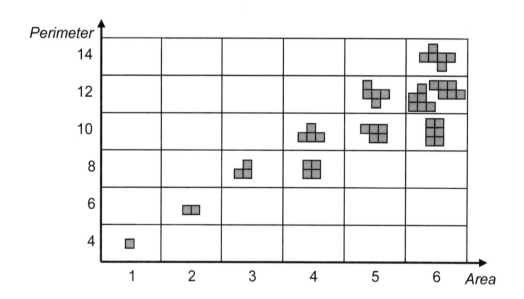

This representation can encourage learners to ask more questions: What is the greatest/smallest number of tiles that can be used to make a polyomino with a given perimeter? What is the greatest/smallest perimeter of a polyomino made with a given number of tiles?

> **PowerPoint**
>
> PowerPoint 11-1, *Polyomino Scatter Graph*, shows how the Area and Perimeter Scatter Graph may be built up and used to draw conclusions about the properties of the shapes.

c) Median, Mode and Mean

As well as collecting and representing data, learners may need to process it, for example by finding the median, mode and mean of a set of numbers. The definitions of these concepts, and the procedures to be followed to work them out, are usually presented entirely in symbols, without any pictures or models. So here again, as in so many areas of mathematics, there is a danger that the rules will be learnt by rote, with little understanding – and then forgotten.

But all of these concepts may be represented physically with a set of sticks of interlocking cubes, or tiles, representing the numbers whose statistics are to be found. For example, five numbers, 7, 4, 8, 2 and 9, may be represented with five sticks:

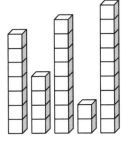

Arranging the sticks in order of height will help learners to see the value of the median – the middle value. In this set of five sticks, the third, which has a height of 7, is in the middle, so the median of this set of numbers is 7.

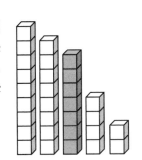

When we have an even number of sticks, however, there is no stick in the middle – so the median must lie halfway between the two middle sticks.

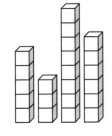

In this set the middle sticks are 6 and 5 cubes high, so the median of these four numbers is $5\frac{1}{2}$.

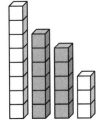

But what about the mean? Well, the mean of a set of numbers is a very simple idea. It is the answer to the question, *What would it be if I shared them all out equally?* Here again, the concept can be demonstrated effectively with sticks of interlocking cubes, or with tiles.

For example, to find the mean of the five numbers, 7, 4, 8, 2 and 9, we again need our five sticks:

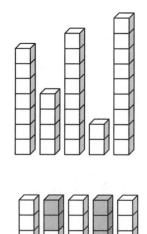

The cubes in the sticks can then be rearranged to even them out, giving five sticks of 6 cubes – so the mean of the five numbers is 6.

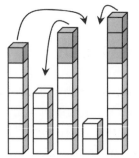

In this case the mean is a whole number – but it clearly need not be. For example, take the mean of 5, 3, 8 and 6.

Most of the cubes can be shared out equally, to give four sticks of 5 cubes each.

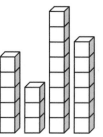

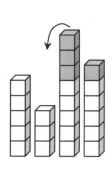

But two cubes will be left over.

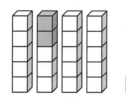

These last 2 cubes must also be shared out. There are 2 cubes to share between four sticks, or an extra half cube for each stick, giving a mean of 4½.
This model helps to explain why the mean of a set of whole numbers may not be a whole number.

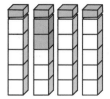

In the Classroom – *Bits and Pieces*

Sometimes non-whole-number means can be surprising. For example,

What is the mean number of brothers and sisters of the learners in the class?

What is the mean number of learners in one class in the school?

What is the mean number of pets per learner?

All of these examples involve working with whole brothers and sisters, or whole learners, or whole pets – but the mean is likely to involve bits of people or animals. Learners may come up with other examples – and the concept of 'sharing out' will help to explain, for example, why in a strict mathematical sense we can say that the 'average' cat does not have four legs!

PowerPoint

PowerPoint 11-2, *Brothers and Sisters*, provides an activity in which learners can collect and record a set of data using interlocking cubes, then process it directly by manipulating the data sticks rather than by calculating with figures.

d) Sample Sizes

Some learners who have difficulty working with graphical representations, and who need numbers to give the data meaning, may be puzzled by statistical diagrams that do not include figures. On the other hand, visual and kinaesthetic thinkers are more likely to be able to draw conclusions from the overall shape of the data, rather than the detailed figures. For instance, these pie charts show the proportions of boys and girls, and the proportions of right- and left-handed learners, in one class.

From these pie charts it is possible to tell, for example, that all the boys could be right-handed, but not all the right-handed learners are boys. But we cannot tell how many boys, or how many right-handed learners, there are in the group. The pie charts could represent a group of any size – a single class, a school, or even the population of a country.

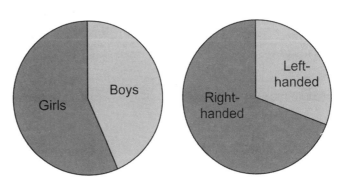

When we are not told how large the group is, however, there is a danger that conclusions may be drawn on the basis of too small a sample. A similar problem may arise when data are presented as percentages. Percentages are convenient because they can be used to compare proportions easily – it is difficult to tell immediately whether 132 out of 360 is more or less than 13 out of 30, but it is obvious that 36 $^2/_3$% is less than 43 $^1/_3$%. But because percentages are always out of a hundred, they can convey a totally false impression that there are at least a hundred members of the sample. For example, it is arithmetically correct to say that 3 out of 4 is 75%. But in a statistical context this may not be useful. If three out of a group of four girls can ride a bicycle then all we can really say is that those three girls can, and that one girl cannot, ride. To talk about 'seventy-five per cent' of the girls being able to ride gives a spurious generality to the observation.

The idea that samples need to be big enough to be sure that the results are valid is not easy to grasp. One approach is to find ways to deliberately 'cook' a set of data, by choosing only the left-handed girls and the right-handed boys, for instance, and then seeing what conclusions might be falsely drawn.

Data Handling – Teaching Points

- Data handling lends itself to a more practical approach than other parts of the mathematics curriculum.

- Learners are likely to engage with activities in which they collect, process and represent their own data.

- Some learners' confidence may be undermined by the sheer quantity of numerical data in lists and tables.

- Graphical representations of data can help learners to get beyond the detail of the specific figures to look at their overall shape, and the relationships between the different parts.

- Some data handling activities can involve shapes, or the learners themselves, rather than numerical data.

- The processes of finding the mode, median and mean of a set of data may be represented with models made of interlocking cubes.

- Graphical representations that do not include any figures help to encourage learners to focus on the overall shape of the data. However, both these and data that are presented as percentages may disguise unreliably small sample sizes.

Resources on the CD

Mathematical PowerPoints

PP 11-1 *Polyomino Scatter Graph*

PP 11-2 *Brothers and Sisters*

Further Reading and Resources

Furbles is an invaluable piece of free software created by Alec McEachran that brings real meaning to the different forms of data representation that learners are likely to meet. It may be accessed at Alec's website, Ptolemy, at http://www.ptolemy.co.uk/furbles.

CONCLUSION

This book is about teaching mathematics to learners with learning *differences*. They learn visually and actively, accessing concepts through images and actions rather than through words. They have significant strengths when they are allowed to use them, but for these learners the conventional print-based curriculum may often be inappropriate. So their learning *differences* may, on occasion, lead to learning *difficulties*. But such difficulties are an outcome of inappropriate teaching. The differences are not, in themselves, a cause of failure.

These visual and kinaesthetic learners are likely to benefit from an approach that focuses on the development of models and images that make key mathematical concepts manifest. The ideas and activities described in this book offer examples of this approach, and are designed to help learners to understand, not just the *how*, but also, crucially, the *why* of mathematics. Teachers may draw on these suggestions to develop materials that will support their own learners' understanding.

Of course, nobody uses only one thinking style. The great majority of learners in most classrooms do access much of the curriculum more or less effectively through the conventional auditory channels. But an approach that focuses on the use of 'models to think with' to develop learners' understanding of mathematics is likely to help all the learners in the group. We all know that *If it's good for special, then it's good for mainstream*. But even more significant here is the inverse: *If it's bad for mainstream, then it's bad for special*. Teaching that relies on the learners' acquisition of meaningless algorithms will serve the highest achievers poorly – but for those in the 'bottom set' it can be a disaster.

As they stand, the philosophy, ideas and materials in this book are just yet more print. The dynamic images on the accompanying CD may help to bring some of them to life – to make them active as well as visual – but if they are to serve any purpose at all then they must be worked on and developed by the learners. And that is down to teachers teaching mathematics – in classrooms, in units, at home, wherever they may be. The ability to think and learn visually and actively is not a weakness to be remedied; it is a strength to be exploited. It is not a difficulty to be overcome; it is an opportunity to be seized. It is not a failure to be regretted; it is a success to be celebrated. Let's do it!

Resources on the CD

Poster

P 12-1 *Cartoon*

Further Reading and Resources 📖

Ronald Davis, 1995: *The Gift of Dyslexia*. Souvenir Press.
This is the most positive and encouraging book I have ever read about the real strengths and advantages of people who 'suffer' from dyslexia. It is well worth reading, whether or not you are a member of this privileged group!

Julie Kay and Dorian Yeo, 2003: *Dyslexia and Maths*. David Fulton.
Kay and Yeo explain the theory which underlies effective teaching strategies for dyslexic pupils. They offer a range of specific ideas for the classroom, but always making the 'why' as clear as the 'how'.

INDEX